Beating the Powers that Be

Independent Political Movements and Parties of the Upper Midwest and Their Relevance for Third Parties of Today

by
Sean Scallon

PublishAmerica
Baltimore

© 2005 by Sean Scallon.
All rights reserved. No part of this book may be reproduced, stored in a retrieval system or transmitted in any form or by any means without the prior written permission of the publishers, except by a reviewer who may quote brief passages in a review to be printed in a newspaper, magazine or journal.

First printing

At the specific preference of the author, PublishAmerica allowed this work to remain exactly as the author intended, verbatim, without editorial input.

ISBN: 1-4241-0366-5
PUBLISHED BY PUBLISHAMERICA, LLLP
www.publishamerica.com
Baltimore

Printed in the United States of America

To Chronicles Magazine and The Rockford Institute for the wisdom

To Justin Raimondo for the inspiration

And to my wife Georgina for all her love and patience

Contents

Introduction 7
Chapter 1 — Last of a Dying Breed 13
Chapter 2 — Building blocs 40
Chapter 3 — The Non-Partisan League 66
Chapter 4 — The Farm Labor Party 89
Chapter 5 — The Progressives 122
Chapter 6 — Back to the Future 157
Conclusion — The New Politics 183
Bibliography 189

Introduction

Many people who subscribe to *Chronicles: A Magazine of American Culture* - the in-house publication of the paleoconservative think tank The Rockford Institute of Rockford, Illinois - like to say it's the college education they never had. Certainly I've felt the same way ever since finding my first copy tucked in the back of the magazine stand at the Book Word store smack dab on Main St. of Shawano, Wisconsin, where I had worked as writer for the local daily newspaper, the *Shawano Leader*, back in 1997.

Chronicles was gracious enough the open the doors of not just opinion journalism to myself, but also art, literature, culture, philosophy and politics in a way that was new and relevant to my then formless beliefs. It was with great excitement that I was able to scrape up enough bucks to attend the Institute's fourth annual summer school with the topic: The American Midwest, Studying its Literature, Poetry, Storytelling and Politics in July of 2001.

Framed as it was against the disastrous day of Sept. 11, the experience of all of us who attended the week-long session was very pleasant memory. In such a memory included the informative lectures given by *Chronicles* writers and editors, the field trip to the nearby homes of acclaimed Wisconsin author Sterling North and poet Lorine Niedecker and the wonderful sunset fish boil at the Buckhorn Supper Club on the shores of Lake Koshkonong.

It was this summer school, patterned on the summer seminars the great scholar and author Russell Kirk used to hold on his Piety Hill farm in Mecosta, Michigan, that gave birth to this book. The idea came from lectures given by Antiwar.com editor and founder Justin Raimondo on "Populists and Progressives," that were an integral part of the Midwest's political milieu for the first half of the 20th century. The title came out a movie recommended to me by another lecturer, author and University of Wisconsin-Superior English professor Anthony Bukoski, called *Northern Lights* which detailed the rise of the Non-Partisan League of North Dakota in the background of the every day struggles of Norwegian farmers against the weather, foreclosures and loneliness of the Plains. "Beating the powers that be" was a line heard right away in the opening minutes of the film, which won an award at the Cannes Film Festival of 1979, and was something the farmers and laborers of the Upper Midwest did quite often through the independent political movements and parties they helped to organize and support.

Other ideas and inspirations came from one of the few books I've read in the last few years that I enjoy looking through again and again any time I can get my hands on it. Kevin Phillips' *The Cousins' Wars* details the rise and dominance not just of the English speaking world but also of its consensus ideals of free markets, centralization, political liberties and individualism through three main wars: the English Civil War, the American Revolution and the War Between the States. It is a fascinating look at how these wars shaped the settlement, economy, culture and political divisions of much of American history with detailed studies of the various Anglo ethnic and religious groups. And Phillips did not stop at 1865. His last chapters deal with the rise in contention of the German and Nordic-speaking world of the Midwest and West to Anglo world of the East and South and how the English-speaking world had triumphed again by the end of World War II. These chapters too were detailed with voting patters and support levels for various movements and parties among the ethnic German and Scandinavian populations of the Middle West. It is in the same spirit and style of *The Cousins' Wars* that Beating the Powers that Be is written.

The biggest realization to my thinking that the Rockford Institute, *Chronicles*, and *The Cousins' Wars* brought forth is how culture dominates our politics. Which lever a person will pull in a voting booth, which "X" we mark on a ballot or which chad we decide to leave pregnant, is greatly determined by who are family and friends are, where we work, where we went to school, where we go to church if we go at all, what vehicles we drive, what books we read and so forth. Far from being individualists, the American electorate votes in communities of interest and always has since the dawning of the Republic when the merchant class of New England supported the Constitution and the landed gentry of Virginia opposed it. If this was not true, then John Zogby, Celinda Lake, Frank Luntz, Stanley Greenberg, Mark Penn and Bill McInturff, to name just a few prominent pollsters, would all be out of business. This realization is also why most third parties (a generic term since the United States has any number of parties from the two major ones down to the smallest Trotskyist sect) fail to make much of an impact on the broader electorate and why the three independent political parties of the Upper Midwest: the Non-Partisan League of North Dakota, the Farm-Labor Party of Minnesota and the Progressive Party of Wisconsin, did have success. These political parties combined their socialist ideologies with appeals to culture, language, reform, economics and religion to create swaths of support bigger than a mere ideological party could ever hope to do.

There have been many detailed books and other works of scholarship written on the history of these three independent political parties. What my writing looks at is the cultural and economic factors within the Upper Midwest that made the success of these parties possible, connecting the ties of ethnicity and religion and employment together as Phillips did in *The Cousins' Wars*. There will also be chapters that deal with each specific party and the states they represented along with a chapter on the late U.S. Senator Paul Wellstone who was, in many ways, the last link between the populist and progressive past of the region and today. Within each chapter will be a section on topics that link each of these parties and movements together, such as the populist style, their influences on national politics, their critiques of U.S. foreign policy and their decline in the face of the nationalization of the Democratic Party. The final chapter deals with examples of those political parties and movements outside the dominant two-party system in our nation today and how they have been able to work effectively within the same system.

The failure of the Reform Party to break into American politics as a significant third force during the 1990s and the continued languishing of other non-major parties in obscurity, ineffectiveness and irrelevance, was a missed opportunity. But other opportunities will come along in politics and non-major parties and movements can take advantage of them if they are able to structure themselves based on culture as much as they are about ideology. This was the hope I had writing my first article for *Chronicles* on the subject two years ago ("Non-Partisanship" *Chronicles*, February 2002) and that hope continues with this more extensive work.

Persons I would like to thank for their help in this project include those who were gracious to give of their time for interviews. From Wisconsin: Robert Dueholm and Marguerite and JoAnn Hallquist; From Minnesota: Hy Berman, Dane Smith and Lisa Pattni; From North Dakota: Lloyd Omdahl and David Danbom from my previous research on the Non-Partisan League and Bill Kretschmar; Nationally: Stephen Moore of the Club for Growth, Jim Clymer of the Constitution Party, Ben Manski of the Green Party, Thomas Naylor of the Second

Vermont Republic and Dr. J. Michael Hill of the League of the South.

I would also like to thank the employees and staff at the *Inter-County Leader* newspaper in Frederic, Wisconsin; the State Historical Society of Minnesota in St. Paul; the North Dakota State University Library in Fargo and to the public libraries in Menomonie, Wisconsin and Red Wing, Minnesota for their help in the research portions of this project.

And finally I would like to thank my family and friends for all their support and encouragement in this, my first attempt at authorship.

Sean Scallon, January 2005

Chapter 1—Last of a Dying Breed

The trip to the Iron Range was like many he had taken before, so much so that some people had referred to this distinct place as his "second home"[1] from his one in the Twin Cities. He had been to fairs and graduations up here, to union halls and senior citizens centers. He had met with, talked to, spoke, cajoled, sometimes angered but also inspired, mediated, comforted and above all helped persons living on the Range from his job as a U.S. Senator. A bond between the man and the region was formed as strong as the iron found in ground here that's turned into the nation's steel. That it happened here, of all places, made it even more tragic.

The occasion for this latest journey was more somber than a local festival or caucus meeting. A funeral for the father of a friend brought him, members of his family and staff up north again. Paul Wellstone was joined by his wife Shelia, daughter Marcia along with campaign workers William McLaughlin, Mary McEvoy and Thomas Lapic. The pilots of the chartered Beechcraft King Air A100, Capts. Richard Conry and Michael Guess, were trying land the plane through an icy fog that enshrouded the Eveleth-Virginia Municipal Airport. Visibility was reduced to two miles due to the light snow that was falling that morning in late October, the announcement that another cold Minnesota winter was on its way.[2]

As the pilots thought about landing the plane in such awful conditions, the passengers' thoughts concerned the funeral for Martin "Benny" Rukavina, father to State Representative Tom Rukavina (DFL-Virginia) to be held that morning at Sacred Heart Catholic Church in Virginia. They wanted to be at the side of a colleague and friend from the Range to comfort him in his grief.

But also on their minds was a campaign for re-election that was only days away. It was tough campaign, as it was predicted to be, against the popular Republican former mayor of St. Paul, Norm Coleman. Wellstone was a wanted man in the eyes of national Republicans and what they wanted was his seat in order to take control of the Senate again.[3] So much so that the Bush Administration fixed it so Coleman would run against Wellstone instead for running for governor - which is what he really wanted to run for to begin with - and forced out an already announced candidate, State House Majority Leader Tim Pawlenty, from the field (Pawlenty wound up running for governor himself and won). But Wellstone didn't have to worry about which way the Iron Range was going to vote. Not only was it a Democratic-Farm Labor stronghold, its citizens also turned out to vote in high numbers, sometimes up to 75 percent of its voting population in a region of 100,000 people.[4] He would need every one of those votes to win 12 days into the future. As one of the Senate's most outspoken liberals or, as critics would say, radicals, Wellstone was a polarizing figure in Minnesota politics. Not just between Republicans and Democrats or even liberals and conservatives, but even among fellow members of his own party. Ever since fellow Minnesotan Walter Mondale and his coalition of liberal interest groups was crushed in the 1984 presidential election by Ronald Reagan, the national and even the state Democratic party had been trying to offer a more moderate, more restrained and refined version of itself to sell to voters, especially to voters in the growing suburban communities put off by the Democrats' traditional voting blocs such as labor or minorities.[5] And yet here was Wellstone being the skunk of the party. He didn't turn away from such groups, he embraced them. He didn't tone down his rhetoric; he was incendiary and passionate in his leftism. He was throwback to days of the radical Farm-Labor Party, which dominated the state in the 1930s with its coalition of farmers and union laborers across Minnesota. [6] Did he not see, those DFL chieftains would complain, that the Depression was over and such politics had no relevance anymore?

The powers that be in the party thought him obnoxious and bullheaded, yet they could not stop him from winning an apparent worthless U.S. Senate nomination in 1990[7] because nobody else wanted it as badly as he did. Running against a popular incumbent, his upset win shocked Minnesota, shocked the nation, even shocked the world eight years before Jesse "The Body" Ventura did so, moving up from being a former professional wrestler to governor of the state. Wellstone won the way a Floyd B. Olson or a Hubert Humphrey, two of the Gopher State's leftist icons, won their campaigns: coalitions of farmers and laborers, city dwellers and town and country residents, students and old folk all across the state with strong African-American, Hispanic and Hmong support thrown in for this period in time.[8] Democrats weren't supposed to win this way anymore and yet, he amazingly did. Not only that, he did it twice by an even larger margin and against the same opponent in his re-election campaign of 1996.

And he was all set to do it again in 2002. But politics was a background thought in the passengers' minds as the plane was nearing its destination and the funeral of a good friend and strong supporter's father awaited. One could say the Iron Range had made Paul Wellstone. He came here first, in 1989, to gauge support for his senatorial campaign. Had he found none here he would have never had bothered to run because he knew it would have been a hopeless cause. He needed the Iron Range. Not just to win elections, but to show skeptics nationwide, among political writers, columnists, pollsters and campaign managers, even among those in his own party, that his coalition could carry the day for the Democrats. He needed to show that he could unite groups of voters of with very different backgrounds into a common cause.

It was shortly after 10 a.m. that the plane made the approach to the runway. But even with experienced and skilled pilots, the weather conditions forced the plane off course. With no control tower at the small, rural airport, there was no one to guide the plane down safely through the fog and light snow. The pilots had to trust their instruments and their experience to try and land. As they guided the plane downward, they found themselves two miles east of the runway. No distress signal was sent because everything was going smoothly until the final approach to the westbound Runway 27. When radio contact was lost with the plane at 10:20 a.m. and fire and smoke were seen off in the horizon in the nearby woods and bogs that surrounded the airport, St. Louis County emergency teams and sheriff's officials sprung into action. An hour and a half later, the rest of the world finally knew what the Iron Range had already known. Their hero, their champion, was dead.

Why it is that the left's heroes are cut down in their prime through tragedy while the right's heroes just seem to fade away as they grow older, is question only God or the ages can answer. Which fate would you rather prefer? Men cut down by tragic events and turned into martyrs and icons but only after hope has been cruelly robbed from their followers or men who go on to live longer, but grow so incapacitated by time and distance that they are unable to keep their visions and beliefs from being warped by their would-be successors? "Either way you look at it," as the old song goes, "you lose." Maybe so, but to lose one's hero by an assassin's bullet or plane crash when all seemed possible just a few seconds before tragedy strikes is far more devastating, mood-altering and revolutionary, one must agree. Particularly for Rep. Rukavina, who suffered both the loss of his father and close friend that very day. You may not lose a cause if a Sen. Wellstone, Sen. Kennedy, President Kennedy or Martin Luther King dies, but you lose the very people who articulated that cause and were its best salespersons, which are hard to almost impossible to replace as the would-be Wellstones found out the hard way. False prophets and messiahs come and go, claiming to speak for that cause, yet never get anywhere or accomplishing anything except for muddying the waters. That just compounds the tragedy. And on top of all that pain, then comes the irony. Wellstone's public career ended in the woods, a place where it began 12 years ago.

A Lifetime of activism

Speaking of irony, it was delicious during the 1988 DFL convention held in Rochester. Downtown the party elite, its leaders and public office holders and most of the delegates for that matter, stayed in the elegant Kahler Hotel and ate at the equally well-to-do Michael's restaurant. North of town, at a public campground, stayed a group of delegates lacking the funds to afford such luxurious accommodations.[9] As a member of the Democratic National Committee, Paul Wellstone could have been with the party brass. But his heart, along with his body, was right by the campfire with his fellow activists, delegates and campaign managers for Jesse Jackson, who were trying to get chosen for delegate slots to the national convention that year.

A white Jew, a professor at a prominent local private college, working for Jesse Jackson?

Given the history of Jackson's anti-Semitic statements, especially in the presidential campaign of four years earlier, and his support for the Palestinian cause, even a fellow leftist like Wellstone was prepared to write-off Jackson as well in 1988. But when the two met that year, Jackson convinced Wellstone to work for him. That's because he put the black power rhetoric and Nation of Islam minister and anti-Semitic racist Louis Farrakhan in the background and emphasized what the two shared in common: that the American middle-class was being squeezed despite the apparent prosperity of the Reagan years, that farmers and factory workers were hurting, particularly in the heartland of the country in states like Minnesota, and by combining such middle class voters with the minority voters that Jackson represented, the Democratic Party could be revitalized again into the nation's majority party.[10]

So with virtually no money or staff or organization to work with at all, Wellstone had to figure out a way to sell Jesse Jackson to what's known as "Greater Minnesota," the land beyond the Twin Cities and its suburbs. That he did so, helping Jackson get 20 percent of the caucus vote that spring and tying him for second place, was considered remarkable in a state that's over 90 percent white. It was due in large part to the contacts Wellstone had made for many years, contacts among farm groups and labor unions, contacts among student groups as well. A whole network was set up thanks in large-part to a lifetime of activism.[11]

Several factors drove Wellstone from James Dean-like rebel while growing up in the Washington D.C. suburbs to committed leftist activist by the time he graduated from college. First was the shabby treatment of a mentally ill older brother at a local institution that put a great deal of strain on his family's finances and emotions. The second was attending the University of North Carolina at Chapel Hill during the height of the civil rights movement on campus during the 1960s and the third was the belief, after becoming a full time professor, that the teaching of the social sciences had no connection with the real world that people off campus lived.[12] He wanted to link academics with social activism the way professors did back during the Great Depression and New Deal years of the 1930s and 40s before World War II and its aftermath, when the Federal government and corporations moved in to make colleges and universities serve their purposes. Of course it also didn't hurt that he grew up in an environment of activism either. His grandfather on his mother's side, Menasha Davishesky, was a garment worker and labor organizer in the Jewish neighborhoods of the Lower East Side of Manhattan. His grandparents on his father's side reportedly died in Stalinist purges and his father Leon Wexelstein, having immigrated to the U.S. to attend college at the University of Washington in 1914, eventually went to work for U.S. Information Agency during World War II as a writer.[13]

So Wellstone threw himself into his new teaching thesis by "grabbing the gusto" as they say. While a graduate assistant at North Carolina, he was involved with a cafeteria workers' strike.[14] After moving to Minnesota in 1969 to teach at Carleton College, a private liberal arts institution in Northfield, he was arrested for participating in sit-in protests against the Vietnam War at a Federal building in Minneapolis. He had called upon one of Carleton's board members, who worked for then Minneapolis-based Honeywell—A corporation antiwar protestors targeted for its making of munitions during the Vietnam War—to resign for committing "war crimes." In the mid-1980s, he was arrested again for another sit-in, this time at a Paynesville bank to prevent farm foreclosures. Also during that time, he walked the picket lines during a bitter and divisive strike at the Hormel meat packing plant in Austin.[15] Some of his colleagues at Carleton were often horrified by Wellstone's activism[16] as they themselves would not be caught dead at a farm rally or inside a labor temple. Luckily for him he had tenure gained from almost being booted off campus in 1974. Only a popular outcry on campus and within the Northfield community kept Wellstone's job from being terminated. Not only was Wellstone beloved on campus, but also throughout its neighborhood as he set up the Organization for a Better Rice County. It was an activist group that dealt with rural poverty and was organized along the lines of the Industrial Area

Foundations set up by the radical Saul Alinsky, who sometimes gave guest lectures to Wellstone's classes. Many students who took courses from Wellstone found themselves working at the Organization for a Better Rice County following the charismatic professor. "It was sort of like a tilt-a-whirl ride," one student said. "It was something to experience." [17]

Fourteen years later, Wellstone found himself facing another toss-out, this time from the Democratic National Committee. In a power play move at the convention, some of the party elites tried to replace Wellstone as one of Minnesota's representatives on the Committee. He was forced to campaign for himself on the convention floor and spoke to the delegates which, like his previous addresses, had been warmly received. He had survived, but was not overly happy with his party. None of the campers were. They saw the party's presidential nominee, Massachusetts Governor Michael Dukakis, and the DFL nominee for the U.S. Senate, state Attorney General Hubert H. Humphrey III, (better known as Skip) the son of the state party's hero and icon, as being too establishment, too unconcerned for the plight of the middle class and working poor and unable to connect with minority voters at any level.[18] They saw them as sure losers, which, as it turned out, they were. Although Dukakis won Minnesota, (with Wellstone working for him as he worked for Jackson) he was beaten soundly by George Bush I across the nation and Humphrey, in a shocker, was crushed by a 15-point margin to incumbent David Durenberger, someone regarded by his colleagues in Washington D.C. as a lightweight in stature and something of a flake.[19]

The campfire gathering by Wellstone and others connected with the Jackson campaign was not a kumbya moment. These persons began to plot for an upcoming U.S. Senate race in two years time. Most political campaigns begin in fancy law offices or boardrooms atop high downtown skyscrapers. This one began as a weenie roast.

Wellstone would make the race. He knew he had the hearts of

many rank and file Democrats and activists, especially in the Twin Cities area. But he needed more, much more support than that if his campaign would even have a prayer of success. He needed to gauge the support of the one place he knew he absolutely had to have on his side in not just any convention or primary election, but also the general. He had to go to the Iron Range.

The bird's-eye view of a taconite mine from Mineview in the Sky outside of Virginia, Minnesota on the Iron Range

Home on the Range

"...What a Ranger looks for in a candidate is a tough fighter. When you are fighting mining companies or fighting in politics you have to be tough, not a laid-back liberal, but someone on the firing line, someone who's going to walk the picket line with you."[20]

DFL activist Gary Cerkvenik knows the Iron Range and knows what the average Iron Ranger wants in a political candidate. But could an ultra-liberal college professor from the Twin Cities be that kind of candidate and attract Cerkvenik and other activists necessary to be able to carry the Range in an election?

On the one hand was Wellstone's labor activism, already preceding him from his picket line walks with striking Hormel workers and sit-ins to prevent farm foreclosures. That would be important as the DFL on the Range is a labor party. This part of northeast Minnesota, a region known as the Arrowhead, gets its identity from the three fields or "ranges" of iron ore, the Mesabi, Vermillion and Cuyuna, which attracted the great steel companies like U.S. Steel to come in and extract it. Iron mining is tough, back-breaking work and the conditions, both at the mines and at home, practically cried out for unionization. Strikes were organized in 1907, 1913, 1916 and 1917. By 1914, the radical Industrial Workers of the World (IWW or "Wobblies") had gained a foothold there. This gave the region an anti-management, anti-corporatist bent that still lingers to this day. Generations of Rangers listen to tales about this or that mining company's attempt to bust unions despite the unionization of the region by the 1930s. The region's history of absentee mine owners, exploitation by Eastern capitalists and the feeling that decisions affecting the Iron Range are made elsewhere, have created the conditions in which the kind of populism made famous by Non-Partisan Leaguer Charles Lindbergh Sr., Farmer-Laborites like Floyd Olson and Elmer Benson and Democrats like Hubert Humphrey easily sellable. [21] And populism seemed to be what Wellstone was selling.

Wellstone's immigrant background was also a plus. Iron Rangers are the sons and daughters of immigrants. The opening of the mines in the late 19th century coincided with an explosion of immigration to the U.S. during that time period, much of it coming from southern Europe like Italy and the Balkan Peninsula. Thus Italians, Serbs, Croats and Slovenes went to work in the mines in the Upper Midwest from the Upper Peninsula of Michigan to the Range.[22] They were joined by Finns from the Oulu and Vasa regions who came too late to gain any of the farmland to the south and west and instead gravitated towards mining and forestry. Such labor intensive jobs plus their own exposure to socialism led to their radicalization and leadership in much of the labor movements on the Range during early part of the 20th century. Italians and the south Slavs tended to favor the IWW while the Finns dealt into more radical syndicalist anarchism.[23] Also coming to the Range were Poles, Irish, Scots, Cornish, and Swedes as well.

But on the other hand, Wellstone took positions on issues that were decidedly not in-line with many Iron Rangers. They were mostly cultural, foreign policy and environmental issues. He was for abortion and homosexual rights when many in the predominantly Catholic region were not. He was against expanded logging in the Superior and other national and state forests in the Arrowhead and was against motorized vehicles in the Boundary Waters Canoe Area Wilderness and other pristine wilderness areas of northern Minnesota while they were for both. His calls for cuts in defense spending didn't jibe with the "God and Country Democrats," as *Minneapolis Star-Tribune* political reporter Dane Smith called them, who were as patriotic and as despising of Communism as they come. While such positions on these issues may have been popular in the liberal environs of the Twin Cities, they were anathema on the Range.[24]

Indeed, liberals from the Twin Cities espousing such views often met for a chilly reception. Donald Fraser, former mayor of Minneapolis and long-time DFL Congressman, lost a primary election in 1978 to former Hubert Humphrey aide and businessman Robert Short because of Fraser's opposition to development in the region. Native son Rudy Perpich, the only Iron Ranger ever elected governor, upset the DFL-endorsed state Attorney General Warren Spannaus in the 1982 primary thanks to a big Iron Range turnout in his favor and because Spannaus favored gun control and Perpich didn't. The Senate candidates Joan Anderson Growe in 1984 and Humphrey III in 1988 did not impress and thus did not get the kind of voter turnout that they needed or the Range's support. Watching the Iron Range split away from the DFL because of such issues mirrored the way white, ethnic, Catholic and blue collar Democrats went away from the party nationally and supported Republicans like Ronald Reagan, the original "Reagan Democrat."

Focusing on such cultural issues was easy back in the 1970s when the steel industry was booming and two-thirds of the miners were able to pay off the mortgages of their small, but solidly built and comfortable homes. Yet when the recession of the late 1970s and early 1980s came around, the situation was quickly transformed. Unemployment by 1982 reached double digits. The mines' workforce plummeted by over 70 percent. Mines on both the Vermillion and Cuyuna ranges were completely closed, leaving only the Mesabi Range left and even there two big mines had shut down. That led to plummeting home values, empty store fronts and food pantries. While the region had recovered somewhat by the late 1980s and beginning the process of diversification, the damage done to local economy by the recession and the exodus of skilled workers and others from the Range was still taking its toll. On top of that, another recession was looming as 1990s had just begun along with the push for free trade and the flooding of U.S. markets of cheap foreign steel. Plus, technological changes and consolidation in the steel industry meant the days when tens of thousands of Rangers worked in the mines were over. [25]

This environment made it a lot easier for Wellstone to come in and make his pitch to local DFL activists and government officials. One of those activists was Lisa Pattni of Virginia.

"His activism really impressed people," Pattni said. "He was a history professor and he knew the history of the Range, knew the struggles and believed that strong unions serve the workers best, which was important because the steelworkers union did a lot of the organizing for the DFL in the fifth senatorial district and set the agenda here. He also knew the populist history of Minnesota from Floyd Olson to Hubert Humphrey and really believed in that tradition and tried to infuse it into his own campaigns." [26]

Having locked up the activists on the Iron Range by 1989 and with his support in the urban Twin Cities thanks to his work with the Jackson campaign, Wellstone pretty much had the DFL nomination in hand, even though party leaders were trying to convince Mondale to come out of retirement and run for the Senate again. When he refused, Wellstone was all they had left to turn to after he brushed aside several opponents at the DFL's 1990 convention in Minneapolis and in the primary. Fine then, they said. Let him embarrass himself against the popular and supposedly unbeatable Republican incumbent Rudy Boschwitz. Maybe a landslide loss will finally shut him up.

In his campaign, Wellstone had promised he would place offices in Greater Minnesota and the Iron Range was on the top of the list to get one. Having used the Range to help him win in 1990, he knew he would need them again and again to be successful in the future. No way was he going let the grassroots support he had here shrivel. In time, his Iron Range office in Virginia, plus his frequent trips to the region to attend fairs, union picnics, high school graduations and other events, even to get away from it all on vacation, led Range to be referred to as Wellstone's "second home." [27]

"Paul loved the Range," Pattni said. "He knew how important the region was to him, not just politically, but also to some of the policies and issues he worked on while in the Senate. They had a real impact here and he knew it. People on the Range also enjoy life and Paul was one to enjoy life as well so there was just a comfortable fit between himself and the people here. He also had enormous amounts of energy. He worked well before you walked into the office door and well after. His wife Shelia, who had her own desk in his Washington office, was very much his partner and allowed him to devote so much time to his job. That work ethic appealed to Rangers too."[28]

Pattni went to work in Wellstone's Virginia office in 1995, seemingly suited for the task. She had been born in Duluth, a second generation American whose grandfather was a Croatian miner (her maiden name is Radosevich) and union organizer from Biwabik, who lived up the North Shore road in Two Harbors before going to college at the Evangelical Lutheran Church-affiliated Augsburg in Minneapolis and studied a year abroad in East Africa. She had lived in Virginia since 1980, seeing first hand the effects of the recession at ground zero. She moved from a job with a local Girl Scouts troop to Wellstone's office in 1995 and found out right away that Wellstone's belief in government action played well on the Range even when it didn't nationally during the time of the Republican Revolution and the GOP's takeover of Congress for the first time in over 50 years.

"People on the Range use a lot of government services and really demand a lot from government," Pattni said. "So it gave our three-person staff a lot of work to do. They are very much connected to the idea of an active citizenship and we would get calls all the time over all sorts of issues."

Wellstone wanted his local offices to be an extension of his activist personality and policies. In this he shared a belief that Robert LaFollette always held that progressivism was about local activism, or "empowerment" of citizens where they lived rather than broad national or international movements. His support of the Minnesota farmer, factory worker, for the PRIG (Public Research Interest Group) movement and consumerist "Nader's Raiders," was in sharp contrast to the progressivism of a Woodrow Wilson or the Roosevelts (both Theodore and Franklin) who favored more broadly based national movements. Thus, issues affecting rural areas, the environment, mining and development became specialties for study by his staffers in order to create policies for legislation the Senator could introduce or work on and know what to vote for or against. They also became places where young activists could intern or have fellowships. And they were a part of the mediation politics that Wellstone practiced so often to keep his electoral coalition in tact.

"Take logging for example," Pattni said. "Paul has been painted as an enemy of logging and an enemy of business by the anti-environmentalists who want to use his strong support for the environment as a wedge issue. We would meet with contract loggers in the region, we would always ask them what their concerns were and what the issues mattered most to them were. We found out that contract loggers often earn low pay and work in dangerous conditions. So Paul would always look for ways to help improve their working conditions and pay. We were always looking for common ground to agree on with different groups. Many of the logging groups, to be honest, were prepared not to like us given what they had heard or what their perceptions were. We were always up front about what we agreed and disagreed on, but again we searched for common ground and worked together on what we agreed with. In this way we could better mediate and find balances between environmentalists and loggers that worked for both sides."

Such work came in very handy by the time Wellstone ran for re-election in both 1996 and 2002. He would use the work had he done with the contract loggers to blunt the charges that he was anti-business or anti-development.

"Paul is the only liberal politician I've seen," Dane Smith said, "who can get the tree-huggers and the loggers, the sportsmen and the outdoor enthusiasts all on his side. That's an amazing ability for any politician, but for someone as polarizing and controversial as he was and with the kind of support he has, it was truly amazing." [29]

That work went alongside traits that all politicians of the populist persuasion seem to have or inherit in their genes.

The Populist Style

The DFL held their 1982 convention at the Duluth Entertainment and Convention Center, popularly know as "The DECC," along the lakefront. As the convention was winding down, the delegates were tired, bored and eager to conclude their business and go home. They were hardly going to be bothered to listen to nominating speeches for the office of state auditor, of all things, and most didn't. They certainly weren't going to pay any attention to a short man with a wild, frizzy afro up there at the podium looking like well dressed hippie. The loud talking among the delegates seemed to drown out what the speaker was saying. [30]

But that speaker made sure his voice rang out over the convention hall. And pretty soon, some people started paying attention. Then some more and still more stopped talking and started listening. Pretty soon the whole of the DECC, delegates and audience members alike, had their ears on to what the speaker was saying and they liked it a lot. It was as though they were in a time warp and there was a young Hubert Humphrey or Eugene McCarthy up on the rostrum firing them up. Or, if they were old enough, they imagined it was Floyd B. Olson, speaking like a preacher to the congregation. And if they were older still, they could imagine a Charles Lindbergh Sr. standing on hay wagon, wowing a crowd of farmers in Stearns County.

As a committed leftist, Paul Wellstone could speak from his heart and speak with passion in what he believed in. Moderates cannot do this because they do not believe fully. They have to count on quiet reasoning to win votes and an audience wishing for quiet, wishing for, well, moderation. But all Wellstone had to sell for himself was his passion and if he could get the delegates to buy into that passion then they were his because the emotion unleashed by that passion would lead them to his favor. And in a scene not seen perhaps since the 1896 Democratic Convention when William Jennings Bryan's "Cross of Gold" speech lifted him to the Democratic Party's presidential nomination, so to, did the delegates in Duluth stampede to Wellstone and he was nominated on DFL ticket (and go down as the only DFLer to lose statewide that year to future governor Arne Carlson).

"Who is that screamer?" Dane Smith asked, reporting on the convention for the *Minneapolis Star-Tribune*. Back then Wellstone came across as a bit terrifying. "I must admit from my vantage point I thought he was pretty scary." Smith said in reflection. [31]

Wellstone should have been thankful the speech wasn't televised, for if it was, it may well have ended his political career right there and then. Politicians who "scream" on television in this day and age as are seen as crazy and mentally imbalanced, as Howard Dean found out the hard way. The small screen shrinks everyone down to size and what plays well in the hall doesn't always come across to viewers at home as passionate and brilliant oratory, especially when the camera focuses close up on your eyes and sees a twinge of madness, or sees the veins bulge on your neck, the sweat pouring from your brow or catches the redness of your flush face. Passionate oratory conjures images of Hitler or Mussolini or Castro's fiery words played over and over again on the History Channel or on public television programs. It's given a bad connotation because some bad people just happened to be great orators.

But before the television age, fiery oratory was a must for a populist politician. If you were a political hack and a bore, you could still get elected with the backing of the machine. But if you were fighting against the establishment, if you didn't have the resources or the money the machine had and the press was against you, then you needed golden oratory to win over the voters. You needed charisma, energy, and charm to bring them on your side. You needed to connect to the voters by living their life stories and feeling at one with them. You needed a different kind of political campaign to overcome all the disadvantages of fighting against the system. Wellstone was a throw back to the age when the independent parties of the Upper Midwest cornered the market on oratory and energy when it came to campaigning.

It's May, 1879, and the University of Wisconsin campus in Madison is all abuzz, waiting for a train to arrive from Iowa City, Iowa. Brass bands are ready to strike up and confetti is waiting to be thrown in the air waiting for their hero to come into the station. No, it wasn't a member of the Badgers' football or basketball teams (not even official sports then at UW), but a member of the school's public speaking team, coming back from a contest at the University of Iowa with a championship in hand for his presentation of Iago from Shakespeare's Othello. [32]

Even before his public career began, Robert LaFollette Sr. was considered a gifted and well-renowned orator as his reception back in Madison showed. When he became a lawyer and then Dane County District Attorney, that reputation grew and grew. So much so, that he was invited to give speeches at Fourth of July festivals, churches, poetry readings and plays. He made a great deal of income from speaking on the "Chautauqua" circuit around rural American, mass meetings in open tents or halls which included speakers of adult education and performers of entertainment that were a part of the progressive culture of that time.[33] His attorney's form of oratory, accentuated with a prosecutorial manner of indictment at the corruption he found in state government and in Washington D.C. overwhelmed his opponents and sold itself well not just to the well-educated of Dane County but to farmers, merchants and working men all across the state. It gave him a charisma that allowed him to be elected governor and U.S. Senator, led to a following for him in the state and across the country, allowed him to run for president and be able to transfer that legacy on to his sons so they could form the Progressive Party back in the 1930s.

As a tall 6-2, blue-eyed and handsome young Scandinavian, Floyd B. Olson was going to attract a look from any crowd he was speaking to. But more than just looks, Olson could connect with rural and urban audiences for the lifetime experiences both shared. Before he became a lawyer, Olson worked several jobs from salesman to fisherman, miner and longshoreman. One of his salesperson jobs required him to sell Bibles for the Vin Publishing Company in southern Minnesota. That allowed him to occupy church pulpits and perfect his style by delivering sermons. He also sold farm machinery in Canada. When he spoke in favor of worker's rights or the farmer's plight, he spoke from the heart and from the head for he knew what he was speaking about and could deliver it with a passion for the experiences he had and the people he knew and met along the way. [34]

So formidable was his oratory that former CBS newsman and commentator Eric Severeid, who attended the University of Minnesota during Olson's term as governor, described him as a better orator than even Franklin Roosevelt. [35] Certainly the audiences were spellbound as this article from the *Minneapolis Journal* described an Olson speech: "...Those standing stood like statues from start to finish. Those sitting sat forward on the edge of their chairs, intent not to miss a word." [36]

A nickname like "Wild Bill," can mean a lot of different things, but for William Langer, also known as "Mr. Bang," it meant a rambunctious speaking style as well. Like LaFollette and Olson, Langer too was a lawyer as well, DA in Morton County and then elected North Dakota Attorney General in 1916 on the Non-Partisan League ticket. He could connect with voters because he could speak their language. In this case, it was German, the language of the *Volksdeutchen* as he was one of them born of Bohemian-German immigrants in 1886 in Casselton, ND. Combined the two and Langer was a popular person to hear speak in southern North Dakota where most of the Volkdeutschen live. Bill Kretschmar, a lawyer in Ashley who serves in the North Dakota state House of Representatives and was its former speaker, grew up during Langer's political heyday in the 1930s. His family, quite prominent in the local politics and business in the area, knew Langer well.

"No question his being able to speak German helped him in this area," Kretschmar said. "He'd be here in Ashley and Wishek and other German areas quite a bit. Besides that, it also helped that he was a pretty rambunctious speaker. He was a thunder and lighting kind of speaker and knew how to get a crowd going. Remember this was the era before microphones and electric sound systems, so talking louder than the next person was a must in the politics of that time." [37]

Langer was also skilled in the art of personal politics. Good constituent services, like those provided by Wellstone, allowed him to identify with the "little guys" by helping them deal with the Washington bureaucracy, whether it was a lost Social Security check or obtaining veterans benefits or promoting local candidacies for federal judgeships. Langer would always send greeting cards for holiday occasions and answered every letter he got and solicited opinions from his constituents as well.

Along side their speaking prowess, Langer, Olson and LaFollette and his sons all built grassroots political organizations from the ground up to serve their campaigns and the parties built around them. They had no other choice after eschewing support from the major parties. The personal charisma and energy they exuded was all they had and it was vital to draw people to their standards. Such followings often times led to political arrogance and stubbornness and in extreme cases (especially with Langer) abuse of power either by themselves or by the parties that had coalesced around them that ultimately came to be their undoing. Perhaps this was inevitable. The local organizations were there, the conditions that led to political protest, anger and desire for change were there as well. What was needed were leaders to shape and mold these forces into a cohesive political platform and organization. It could have never happened by chance or with lesser men. So it was with Wellstone. By 1990, political unrest was there in Minnesota, the grassroots activists were there as well. All that was needed was someone to bring it all together and Wellstone felt he knew how to do it.

After Wellstone had been elected, the leftist *Mother Jones* magazine called him the "First 1960s radical to be elected to the U.S. Senate." [38] This, of course, is a silly statement. For Wellstone would have never had been elected, much less have even one ounce of support, had he advocated violent takeovers of universities, overthrowing the U.S. government, bombings, or extolled the glories of Maoism while the Chinese Communists were slaughtering millions. Instead, Wellstone visited practically every little café in every little Minnesota town. He didn't just talk to the owners or the customers, but also the waitresses, the dish washers, the short-order cooks, even somebody coming in from the parking lot. He would travel from café to café in a beat up, decrepit and just plain dirty school bus painted green to match his campaign colors. He said he stood up for the "little fellers" against the "Rockerfellers." [39]

"The bus is the symbol of everything that is not slick," Wellstone said, "everything that is not big money. The bus is a campaign tool to the people of Minnesota." [40]

In purposely running a flea bag, non-professional campaign based personal activism and rumpled looks, he had a perfect foil to run against in Rudy Boschwitz. In many ways the ideal Republican, Boschwitz was German-Jewish immigrant who had built himself a home-improvement business called Plywood Minnesota that made him quite well-known around the state.[41] This helped him get elected over the incumbent Wendell Anderson, the former governor and golden boy of Minnesota politics who royally screwed up when he resigned and had his lieutenant governor, Rudy Perpich, appoint him to Walter Mondale's Senate seat when the later was elected vice-president in 1976.[42] The move was a symbol of the political arrogance of a DFL party that had been too dominant for too long and Boschwitz took advantage of it. He whipped Anderson and ended what was once a promising political career in 1978, the infamous "Election Night Massacre" where the GOP had won both U.S. Senate seats, the governor's office and the state House of Representatives, a total triumph for the party not seen in 40 years. Boschwitz had carved out a moderate-to-conservative voting record for himself in the Senate and that, plus the still positive image he had from his business, helped him get re-elected easily in 1984. Boschwitz's star began to rise further when he was named chairman of the National Republican Senatorial Committee and spent much of his time out of state during his second term raising money for GOP Senate candidates. He wasn't around during the height of the farm crisis in the state in the mid-1980s, nor during the divisive Hormel strike of 1985 or dealt with the economic problems of the Iron Range either. The resentment Wellstone knew was out there, especially in Greater Minnesota, Boschwitz was blind to.

Make no mistake that Wellstone ran a class warfare campaign against Boschwitz. When he campaigned for universal health care and more taxes on the wealthy, it was in the Upper Midwest populist tradition to attack the well-to-do and the powerful to the benefit of those who weren't, as Olson, LaFollette or Langer would do the same in calling for a moratorium on farm foreclosures, a state-run grain elevator or a progressive income tax.

He also did so because late Lee Atwater, the great Republican political consultant, would have done the same thing if he was Wellstone's campaign manager. A working man's son growing up in South Carolina, he knew their resentments and fears along with their hopes and dreams as well. He played the class card as well as anyone, just ask Mike Dukakis. He skillfully took George Bush I, the son of a U.S. Senator, Ivy League grad and former ambassador, CIA Director and member of a rich and powerful family and turned him into a man of the people, complete with pork rinds, the PTL Club and country music. He did so not only because he was facing perhaps the worst modern presidential nominee any major party has ever nominated, but also because he knew that conservatives were as class conscious as anyone. With no old money to fall back on nor any connections to power elites on the East and West Coasts, conservatives constantly worry about their status in society (that's why a class sensitive Richard Nixon had so much appeal to this group) and their economic security. They feared not just the poor or even the rich, but their liberal competitors within the upper-middle class, those who were well educated and worked in the professional trades and government, the managerial "New Class," so to speak. They felt this class, born out the baby boom after World War II, many whom were protestors in the 1960s and now were professors in elite universities and colleges (people like Paul Wellstone for example), did not share common values about America and were decadent in areas such as morality, crime, welfare and the defense of the country during the then raging Cold War. Atwater played these themes beautifully against Dukakis and two years later, Wellstone was determined not to let the same thing happen to him. He did so by going after Boschwitz's wealthy image and against the inequities of the Reagan Administration's economic policies in the Upper Midwest.

Of course Boschwitz tried to tag him as an ivory tower elitist and a radical college professor all throughout the campaign. But Wellstone blunted these charges in several ways. One was the common touch he had through all the activism with blue collar voting groups like farmers and workers. Another was his background as a wrestler. Wellstone was a star wrestler in high school at 103 pounds and finished second in the state of Virginia as a sophomore and junior and third as a senior. He attended the University of North Carolina on a wrestling scholarship and coached wrestling at Carleton as well.[43] In a wrestling-mad state like Minnesota, home to a popular high school state tournament in St. Paul that Wellstone always attended; home to NCAA wrestling champions Augsburg College and the University of Minnesota and home to such professional grappling legends like Verne and Greg Gagne, "Jumping" Jim Brunzell, Ric Flair, Larry and Curt Henning, "Ravishing" Rick Rude, Ole and Arn Anderson, Ken Patera and of course, Jesse "The Body" Ventura, Wellstone's wrestling knowledge and interest gave him a common touch most profs would have not have had otherwise. And of course Wellstone's campaign itself, with its dilapidated bus, low budget in comparison to Boschwitz's and grassroots activists running around all over the state, hardly made him look like a "limousine liberal."

"Try not to separate the life you live from the words you speak,"[44] was one of Wellstone's mottos and in so doing, he had shielded himself from Boschwitz's attacks and those of other Republicans and conservatives from 1990 throughout his career. Even when Wellstone forced himself to run TV commercials, his café campaign not reaching the amount of voters needed to be effective, they had quirky, non-slick flair to them that made them interesting and entertaining to watch and were different in tone and style from the slick ads that flooded Minnesota and nationwide airwaves in 1990.[45] Voters were looking for something different from their politicians that year and Wellstone tapped into that mood that ultimately led to the Ross Perot's presidential campaign of 1992.

It was campaign a populist could appreciate because it was all so understandable and real and familiar. If Olson and Humphrey and Lindbergh had been alive to see it they would have recognized it instantly. Wellstone didn't run a Democratic campaign for Senate. That had been tried and failed in the past. Instead he ran a Farm-Labor campaign, against the establishment, against the powers that be, both in his own party and nationally. The campaign he ran got him to at least the point of competitiveness with Boschwitz, so when the heat was on for the incumbent, he began to make mistakes that turned off voters, including writing a letter to Jewish groups questioning whether Wellstone was a "good Jew" or not.[46] Actually, the key swing vote was not those in the middle or even so-called independents, but those who hadn't turned out much before or hadn't turned out to vote in the recent past. They came out again thanks both to Minnesota's same-day registration law and because Wellstone's campaign gave them a reason to come out to the polls once again.

"Wellstone tapped into that prairie populism, the 'little fellers vs. Rockerfellers' instinct and impulse that's always been a part of Minnesota politics since the days of the Non-Partisan League and the Farm-Labor Party in one shape or form," Dane Smith, who chronicled Wellstone's campaign along fellow *Star-Tribune* political reporter Doug McGrath in the book Professor Wellstone goes to Washington. He also tapped into the moralism, sense of justice and high purpose of politics since the days Minnesota was settled by religious New Englanders and pious Scandinavians.[47] As a professor of history and sociology, he knew those veins were deep inside the Minnesota political psyche. All he had to do was mine them out.

What could have been

The future is place in time that often set by emotion. Nostalgia is the emotion of love for the past. Put the two together, and you get the dreamy and speculative "what could have been."

What could have been if Wellstone had lived, if his plane touch downed safely at the Eveleth-Virginia Municipal Airport? Of course, Wellstone could have easily died in plane crash in 2003, but you don't think about such things when you engage in "what could have been." And even if that had happened, history still would have been changed.

Although other objective observers may not say so, this writer feels it is safe to say Wellstone would have won in 2002. It would have been close, but he would have won, defying the Republican trend of that year and overcoming a broken promise to only serve two terms (he felt that the closeness of the balance of power between the two parties in the Senate compelled him run again.) He was starting to open up a lead over Coleman in the polls by that time and most Minnesotans respected, even if they didn't agree with, his vote against the resolution to authorize war in Iraq he cast that year. That fact plus the mobilization of his field army of volunteers in the thousands, bigger than any candidate in the country, would have given him an edge. So formidable was Wellstone's organization that many DFLers hoped he would be able to pull the entire ticket to victory across the state. Thus, the devastating impact his death had upon the whole party contributed somewhat to the DFL's poor performance that year at polls, although, as we will see later, other factors played an even bigger role.

With another Senate victory in hand, what would have been next for Wellstone? Run for governor? He thought about it in 2002 and had he done so he would have been a part of one of the greatest gubernatorial elections in U.S. history against Coleman and Ventura. But being a senator allowed Wellstone to play the role of prophet, sometimes scolding, sometimes cajoling and always forecasting a bright future, as this line from a speech so clearly shows: "We can do better than that. There's a new world in the making and there's a potential for politics to be improving people's lives." Being governor means mostly being a manager, a bean counter and telling people, the very people who support you, no when you have to cut their budgets in order to balance the state's. So running for governor was not really in any future plans. Perhaps run for president? He made an exploratory bid to run for the White House in 1999, but decided against it due somewhat to family concerns, due in other parts to his health (he had been diagnosed with MS) and largely due to the fact Al Gore had the Democratic Party's nomination in 2000 all sewn up when he vigorously defended President Clinton during the impeachment trial. He would have been foolhardy to run then.

But what about 2004? Could he and not Howard Dean been able to mobilize the far left wing of the Democratic Party onto his side? Could he not have reached out from that wing to other interest groups in the party as he had done so effectively in Minnesota, to minorities, public employee unions and blue collar workers the way John Kerry ultimately did and the way Dean, because of his cultural baggage, could not? Could he not have easily and much more effectively work with someone like Joe Trippi, who would have introduced him to internet campaign fundraising to raise the kind of money Dean did to fund his campaign? Could he have not have gotten along better with Trippi? Could he not have found native Iowans enthusiastic enough to make the final push the weekend before the caucus instead of Dean's imports? Would Dean have even run with Wellstone in the race and would have Kerry been able to beat next door neighbor Wellstone in the Iowa caucuses? Would he even have run there at all against Wellstone's presence? And if Wellstone became the nominee could he not have appealed to the very blue collar patriotic, values driven voters that he always appealed to on the Iron Range the way Kerry could not in the general election? The problem, it seems, with modern American liberalism is that there's too many John Kerrys and not enough Paul Wellstones.

History has robbed us a chance to answer all these questions. It's fun to speculate, but also painful too given what a man of Wellstone's considerable talents and energy could have accomplished. Needless to say, Wellstone clearly understood the building blocks the Democrats needed to carry the state and the nation for that matter and built his campaigns on those foundations when others scoffed at him. They were the foundations in Minnesota lain by Ignatius Donnelley, John Johnson, Charles Lindbergh, Floyd Olson, Elmer Benson and Hubert Humphrey years before they had been abandoned over time for other foundations and political building blocks that proved to be chimeras. Sadly, Wellstone has turned out to be the last of a dying breed because others who have tried to match his populist style and methods of grassroots campaigning haven't been too successful because they either lacked the common touch he had, the magical oratory, the sense of history, love of life and shared optimism. He's also the last of a dying breed because those very foundations and building blocks are crumbling away and changing so rapidly that they can't win elections anymore all by themselves. New foundations will be built but they won't be done with Wellstone, or any of the ghosts of the populists and independent parties of the Upper Midwest that he now joins, in mind.

Chapter 2—Building blocs

Perhaps no one summed up better the reasons why Americans vote in the ways that they do than acclaimed writer and reporter Theodore White did in his book *America in Search of Itself: Pursuit of the Presidency 1956-1980:*[2]

"Competition is one of the engines that drives television news; from this competition have come many of the most daring forward steps of television reporting. My first exposure to such competition came on the night of the midterm elections of 1962.

Two personalities were to emerge that night. The first was a newcomer, Louis Harris, an intense and dedicated pioneer of numbers who combined the qualities of a scholar and an entrepreneur. Harris had come aboard only recently at CBS, but as a man of imposing reputation. He had been one of John Kennedy's senior advisers in the 1960 campaign, the first personal polling "strategist" of modern campaigns. More important, he had an idea: It was that the story of an election was not told by the totals of the vote; the story of an election lay in how the votes broke down. He had by that night cost CBS some seventy thousand dollars-then a huge sum-making "models" of eight major states, dissecting them into key precincts, precincts of blue-collar voters, white-collar voters, suburban voters, rural voters, big-city voters, Catholics, Protestants, Jewish and black voters. Americans, he felt, voted by communities of interests. Dissect the communities, he felt, and you could not only predict the results, but explain it. Harris had posted 80 observers who were to telephone in precise counts from "pure" precincts - all black, all white, all Catholic, all Jewish - all together reproducing the regional, income and ethnic patterns that made the mosaic of the nation.

Both Harris and I were attached to CBS' newly contrived "election unit." Enormously expensive, it had been the counterstroke to NBC devised by Richard Salant, then president of CBS News and Blair Clark, its general manager...California, where Richard Nixon was running against Governor Edmund Brown, was the most important race that evening. I kept insisting we could not call the race until San Francisco's votes were in - San Francisco always offset Los Angeles in California, just as Cook County offset "downstate" in Illinois. The polls had just closed. Harris, a good friend, treated me as if I were as obsolete as Mark Hanna. It was over, he said. The samples from his key precincts were in his hand; Nixon was licked. In the background brooded Blair Clark, an incurable Puritan. Clark had committed the money for this experimental election unit, but he felt it was wrong to divide Americans into blacks and whites, Protestants and Catholics, Jews and Gentiles. Yet the operational authority to make the call was in the hands of Leonard, later to become president of CBS News himself. His election unit would grow over the years to a corps of scholars and experts as large as any university's department of political science. Leonard, controlling the "call," called Harris over White, thus for Brown over Nixon. From Leonard, the word passed upstairs to the second star of the evening, Don Hewitt, senior executive producer of the night. He, like Leonard, would go on to greater things.

I slipped upstairs to the control booth. Hewitt was "networking." He was like the admiral of an aircraft carrier, surveying his feeds on the telescreens, absorbing intelligence from Leonard and Harris below, talking to Walter Cronkite, the anchorman - but also, like an admiral, scrutinizing the enemy, watching the monitors on his two rivals, NBC and ABC. And at this moment Hewitt struck - Cronkite announced that CBS declared Brown the winner over Nixon in California. Hewitt swiveled in his chair to watch his monitor of the chief enemy, NBC. David Brinkley was on. Obviously NBC was monitoring CBS just as CBS commentators were doing. Brinkley visibly winced as his earpiece told him CBS' call. Hewitt chortled "…wry that one you son of a bitch, try and wry that one!"

All through the night, as Harris' demographic breakdowns proved accurate in state after state, CBS was ahead, NBC catching up. What was happening, there in the studio, seemed moderately important, even exciting; the true importance was to come later. Politicians, who had always known that Americans voted by communities of interest, now saw, clearly, that computers could define such interests, measure them, build predictions and strategies on them. If a major network could talk about such matters publicly, politicians too could plan, precisely, on the interaction of these communities."

The realizations that came to Teddy White that election night back in 1962 were known already. Politicians knew such things about their trade for a long time, each passing down such secrets and methods of vote gathering from, say Mark Hanna's day to Lou Harris and beyond. And one did not have to be some corrupt political hack handing out Christmas turkeys in an Irish neighborhood for a big city political machine to understand it either. The organizers of Non-Partisan League, the Farm-Labor Party and the Progressives knew it too.

"Make the rubes pay their goddamn money to join and they'll stick - stick 'til hell freezes over…Find out the damn fool's hobby and then talk it. If he likes religion, talk Jesus Christ; if he is against the government, damn the Democrats; if he's afraid of whiskey, preach prohibition; if he wants to talk hogs, talk hogs. Talk anything he'll listen too, but talk, talk until you get his goddamn John Hancock to a check for six dollars." [2]

Non-Partisan League organizer and founder Arthur C. Townley may have been quite cynical when he said this to his NPL field organizers, but he knew, nonetheless, how people voted and it did not require a computer to tell him. Although, for a Harris, Hanna or Townley, the times they worked in had many voters who could not say a word of English nor even read in their own native tongues, let alone be caught up in the politics of this strange new world. The political party, the machine, or whatever you want to call it, was their only guide to participation in America's government. Nowadays, with a better educated mass of voters (and with TV networks not even bothering to wait for the final precinct count to be tallied to declare a winner) such organizations are not needed to play this role and thus party loyalty is no longer the same.

But perhaps this anecdote describes the average U.S. voter today: In conversation with a relative of my wife at a wedding party he described his method of voting: Democrat for most offices on the ballot unless he happened to really like or knew or preferred a Republican in particular race. Indeed, there may be voters who put in a great deal of time and thought and study over a particular campaign, the issues involved and the candidates themselves, but they are a small minority in this 24/7 world. When you're alone in the voting booth, and you're trying to decide whether candidate X or candidate Y can examine a dead body better than the other, which party they belong to becomes a nice shortcut when voting for the county coroner.

Two for America

The modern two-party system began in 1796 when Thomas Jefferson and James Madison, two men who represented the landed gentry of the South, traveled north to New York City for a "butterfly hunting expedition." Whatever new specimens of butterflies they were able to find on the Hudson highlands paled in importance to the deal they struck with one Aaron Burr, leader of the Society of St. Tammany.[3] On the surface, the society fought Manhattan's fires through volunteer companies and kept a few a saloons. Go deeper and you'll find that Burr and company were some of the savviest vote getters in the nation.[4] By striking this alliance between two unlikely partners, Jefferson was able to create the political party he wanted to fight against his chief rival, Alexander Hamilton and his Federalists. Thus was born coalition politics, the hallmark of our two-party dominant system.

Like the Constitution, or the Declaration of Independence, or the Bill of Rights, the two-party dominant system of politics has reach institution status in the nation, meaning people may not know all the specifics as to why it is so, but they know it is there, it's good, it's enduring and so it comforts them. Scholars may point to the "first-past-the-post" way we elect candidates instead of proportional representation, or the way the two parties share agreement on nothing else but the fact that they and they alone should dominate political discourse through difficult statewide ballot access laws, control of debates (the two-party run Commission on Presidential Debates) and elimination of innovative voting procedures (the New York state legislature outlawed proportional voting for the New York City Council in 1947 which enabled avowed Communists to get elected.) [5]

But not all of these explanations hold water as to why we are two-party dominant. Other Anglo voting societies like the United Kingdom and Canada have "first-past-the-post" systems as well for Parliament and both have strong traditions of voting for third or even fourth and fifth parties. Ballot access laws vary in degree of difficulty state by state and some states offer public financing to third party campaigns. Third party candidates can at least participate in debates for statewide or local offices on television or radio without affecting their vote totals by a tremendous amount.

Instead, call it a sense of cooperation or maybe even, for this day and age, bigger is better, as to why our political energies are focused into two major parties. Or better yet, let's put it bluntly: candidates and politicians and their supporters and financiers want to win first and foremost. And Jefferson and Madison realized that they could not win, could not beat John Adams and the Federalists, without adding on to the base of their party. By the election of 1800, the alliance Jefferson and Madison struck four years earlier paid off. In May of that year, the Democratic-Republican Party won control of the New York state legislature thanks to Burr and Tammany's efforts in turning out votes for the party in New York City. The legislature picked presidential electors that voted for Jefferson over Adams and a new era in U.S. politics was born. [6]

U.S. political groups, whether ethnic, ideological, single issue or religious, realize quickly that they can have more success in an election, or in making laws that favor their interests, or in dispensing patronage, by working together rather than working alone by themselves. Such groups can mobilize voters, but given the vastness and diversity of the country only to a limited effect. Members of the Christian Coalition, for example, know they could, if they wanted to, form their own separate political party and elect candidates on their own successfully as they have done in the past for the Republicans. Yet they realize that while they may win a few elections here or there, they would have more influence and power in Congress, in the White House, in the governor's or mayor's office working within a major party than being on the outside. On the outside, they would be isolated and seen as unimportant. On the inside they have a voice made loud by the number of votes they can produce as Karl Rove almost certainly knows. And the openness of the major parties (no membership fees one must pay or loyalty oath one must take) allows them their "place at the table" to coin a phrase from the Coalition's first leader Ralph Reed. Or to use another example, Catholics could never have seen one of their own, John F. Kennedy, elected if he ran as the presidential candidate of a purely Catholic political party. As a Democrat, they could.

It should also be pointed out that the two-party system fits the set ups of U.S. business and popular culture as well: three big auto companies, three main breweries, the Big Five accounting firms, five main oil companies and airlines, major and minor league baseball or hockey, major and mid-major conferences in college basketball and so forth. The division between big guys and little guys predominates and those trying to make the jump into the big leagues, from John DeLorean to the USFL (United States Football League) to Ross Perot, find it difficult despite all the cash they have on hand to spend. The two major parties have resources in manpower, organization and access to funds that minor parties could only dream of having. Politics itself is their business which the minor parties find hard to compete with. Thus, such dominance permeates through our entire culture. Children, from the time they start learning about the U.S. political system, learn the two-party system and little else. It becomes ingrained and then feeds on itself. This author knew very little about what the Libertarian Party stood for until he reached college and almost nothing about its history until after college.

One can make a valid argument that the two-party system has served the country well by channeling all its diversity of people, economics and views into two competing factions rather than have them dissolving into multiple political units that could lead to instability and upheaval. This legitimacy makes it hard to almost impossible to dislodge the system short of a nuclear holocaust or asteroid strike on Earth. Even if one of the two majors disintegrates like the Whigs did in the 1850s, another will step into its place, just as the Republicans did. The GOP was only a third party by technicality. Unlike a lot of third parties, it had the support of a significant number of elected officials, a regional base and had financial backing as well.

Know your role to play

Since U.S political parties are not ideological, ethnic or religious vessels by themselves alone, and are in the business of winning elections, this can have the effect of calcifying political discourse. If generals, as it is often said, tend to fight the last wars in the present, then the major political parties latch on to winning formulas and coalitions until they are no longer sustainable. Often times it takes a third party to show that. The majors can also tend to shy away from important debates or fudge issues or even ignore the reality on the ground as to not upset the coalitions they have assembled.

Thus, there are any numbers of roles minor parties can play within the current system, from promoting debate on certain issues, to highlighting the concerns of a particular voting bloc to changing the direction of political discourse. The examples are numerous: Robert LaFollette's Progressives, Floyd B. Olson's Farm-Laborites and Norman Thomas' Socialists helped to steer the Democrats to the left and to the New Deal. Strom Thurmond's Dixiecrats and George Wallace's American Independents steered the GOP to the South, to Christian conservatives and to white ethnics in the Midwest and East. But such success is not by accident. The Libertarians and Constitutionalists have not prevented the Republicans from turning into spendthrift proliferates nor have the Greens prevented the Democrats from passively accepting the United States' occupation of Iraq.

The successful third party, the one that wins electoral votes in presidential campaigns, the one that elects members to Congress and state legislatures and the one that maybe wins even a governor's office, is the one that combines ideology with an approach that targets various voting blocs to its cause and converts them as voters. Parties fitting that bill include the three from the Upper Midwest, the Non-Partisan League, Farm-Labor and the Progressives.

Down on the Farm

The acclaimed Wisconsin author Hamlin Garland was born and raised on a farm near West Salem in what's known as the Coulee region of the state, a land deep gulches between large hills of grass and woods left untouched by the glaciers of the Ice Age. It's perfect for dairy farming, which the state was making its transition to at the time Garland was growing up. But Garland also spent time on farms in the western Plains in Iowa and the Dakotas. He saw first hand the difficult lives of farmers throughout the region and wrote his experiences down in well received books such as *Main Traveled Roads*.

This passage from the book, a short story entitled "Up the Coolly," shows a successful playwright from the Coulee region who left home to seek fame and fortune, coming back to visit his mother and brother on the family farm. It offers a synopsis of Garland's work: [7]

"Howard. - this is my wife," said Grant, in a cold, peculiar tone. Howard bowed toward the remarkably handsome young woman, on whose forehead was a scowl, which did not change as she looked at him and the old lady.

"Sit down anywhere," was the young woman's cordial invitation.

Howard sat down next to his mother and facing the wife, who had a small, fretful child in her arms…The supper was spread upon a gay-colored oil-cloth and consisted of a pan of milk, set in the midst, with bowls at each plate. Besides the pan was a dipper and large plate of bread and at one end of the table was a dish of fine honey.

A boy of about 14 leaned upon the table, his bent shoulders making him look like an old man. His hickory shirt, like Grant's, was still wet with sweat and discolored here and there with grease or the green of the grass. His hair, freshly wet and combed, was smoothed away from his face and shone in the light of the kerosene lamp. As he ate, he stared at Howard, as though he would make an inventory of each thread of the visitor's clothing.

"You see we live just about the same as ever," said Grant, as they began eating, speaking with a grim, almost challenging inflection.

The two brothers studied each other curiously, as they talked of neighborhood scenes. Howard seemed incredibly elegant and handsome to them all with his rich, soft clothing, his spotless linen and his exquisite enunciation and ease of speech. He had always been "smooth-spoken" and he had become "elegantly persuasive"' as his friends said of him and it was a large factor in his success.

Every detail of the kitchen, the heat, the flies buzzing aloft, the poor furniture, the dress of the people, all smote him like the lash of a wire whip. His brother was a man of great character. He could see that now. His gray eyes and rugged face at thirty showed a man of great natural ability. He had more of the Scotch in his face than Howard and he looked much older.

He was dressed in a checkered shirt without vest. His suspenders, once gay-colored, had given most of their color to his shirt and had marked irregular broad bands of pink and brown and green over his shoulders. His hair was uncombed, merely pushed away from his face. He wore a mustache only, though his face was covered with a week's worth of growth of beard. His face was rather gaunt and was brown as leather.

Howard took the little one and began walking up and down the kitchen with her while she pulled at his beard and nose. "I ought to have you, my lady, in my new comedy. You'd bring down the house."

"You don't mean to say you put babies on the stage Howard?" said his mother in surprise.

"Oh yes. Domestic comedy must have a baby these days."

"Well that's another way of makin' a livin', sure." said Grant. The baby had cleared the atmosphere a little. "I' spose you fellers make a pile of money."

"Sometimes we make a thousand dollars a week; oftener, we don't."

"A thousand dollars!" They all started.

"A thousand dollars sometimes, and then lose it all the next week in another town. The dramatic business is a good deal like gambling - you take your chances."

"I wish you weren't in it, Howard. I don't like to have my son—"

"I wish I was in somethin' that paid better than farmin.' Anything under God's heavens is better n' farmin'." Said Grant.

Grant's lament was common then when Garland wrote it as it is now. "Crime Doesn't Pay and Neither Does Farming" is a phrase this writer saw on a bumper sticker once. That's not entirely true. Farming can pay, quite handsomely in some cases. And yet it can rob you blind too. You may be a good farmer and able to produce bountiful harvest or blue ribbon hogs at the county fair, yet if prices are bad you will lose money. All the effort, hard work and sweat you put into your farm will go for naught if the price you sell your grain or cattle for doesn't meet the costs that went into it for fertilizer, feed and fuel, not to mention costs in property taxes, health insurance and hired help as well. And of course we haven't got to the weather yet.

Such variables make farming unique in terms of the number of uncontrollable risks one takes on. The sense of the uncontrollable always shadows a farm operation. The weather, the price of fuel, hog prices in Des Moines, corn futures on the Chicago Board of Trade, government price supports, a record wheat crop in Australia, an American farmer, by himself cannot control any of this and yet all of it in some series of combinations affects the price of what he can sell his commodity for. That price determines if he can pay his bills or have to take an off-farm job, as many do, or have the wife work as well to have her health benefits cover the entire family. What a man cannot control, in spite his best efforts, he becomes frustrated. When frustration sets in, it can lead to anger. And when anger takes over, it either leads to action, or to desperation. There's a fine line between a Gordon Kahl - the North Dakota farmer who blasted two U.S. marshals with a shotgun who were serving an arrest warrant for failure to pay federal taxes on his farm - or the violent Wisconsin milk strikes of 1933-34 and political activism.

Without such anger, it would have been hard for any of the Upper Midwest's independent political parties to form. A candidate can work for the farm vote but often times finds it too diverse to get a handle on. Successful farmers are not going to want to shake up the status quo unlike struggling farmers. Different kinds of farms have different interests when it comes to legislation, or trade deals or environmental laws. It may be the difference between a dairy farm and a row crop farm, or the difference between large corporate operation and a smaller family farm or may even be the difference between an organic farm and one that uses pesticides and genetically engineered seeds. The quality of soil itself could be a divider too. Many farmers that found themselves supporting the Progressive Party in Wisconsin were settled in the "cut-over" districts, those parcels of land in the northern parts of the state cleared of trees during the Upper Midwest's lumber boom of the mid to late 1800s and found the land much harder to work on compared to rich soils of the eastern part of the state where the Progressives were not as strong.[8] Farmers have always found themselves split even by the organizations that represent them. The Farm Bureau tends to be a conservative, Republican leaning group while the Farmer's Union or the National Farmers Organization (NFO), leans more to the left and favors the Democrats. [9]

But when farmers are mad, when they all suffer together at hands of their perceived foes: the milling companies and privately owned grain elevators, the banks, the railroads, anyone they thought was ripping them off despite their honest but back-breaking labor, then they can unite for a common purpose. The first stirrings came in Wisconsin in 1873 when a farmer's organization known as the Grange backed a Democrat named William Taylor and helped him upset Republican incumbent Cadwallader Washburn, one of only four Democratic victories in governor's races from 1857-1958.[10] The Peoples or Populist Party won North Dakota's electoral votes in the 1892 presidential election and fusion candidacies between the Populists and the Democrats elected governors and congressmen in Minnesota and North Dakota during this time period.

But the Populists were ultimately swallowed up by the Democrats, which diminished their appeal in the Upper Midwest for reasons soon explained further in this chapter. For the independent political parties of the Upper Midwest, a much more sturdy foundation was needed in order to organize farmers to their respective causes.

Thus, the cooperative movement became the cinder blocks.

Cooperatives or the shorter, more popular term "co-ops," were founded by weavers in Rochforde, England in 1844 as a way they could band together in their own company to sell their products directly to consumers without the need of middlemen to distribute and market what they made.[11] The idea quickly spread across the water in both directions, through the Atlantic Ocean to New England and through the North Sea to Scandinavia. Since New Englanders and later Scandinavians settled in the states of the Upper Midwest, co-ops followed as well. Co-ops are about democratic and egalitarian principals in business and the ideas that followed included one person, one vote for shareholders, open membership, open records keeping, a limit on returns based on the amount of stock ownership, limits on the number of shares one person could own, an emphasis on returning net margins to customers based on patronage and cash sales at market prices. Business decisions for the co-op, whom to hire and fire, what insurance to purchase and who the board of directors were going to be, were all decided by the shareholders. Meetings minutes were recorded and published in local newspapers.[12]

The co-ops appeal came down to control, the sense that farmers controlled the price and how and when they could market their products. If they could control little else in their business, co-ops at least gave them the opportunity to believe they could be masters of their fate when came to free market's perceived inefficiencies over price and supply. They also helped rural areas for providing markets and market places for goods and offering credit for farmers to buy supplies when the banks would offer none.[13] The only cooperative newspaper in the nation, the *Inter-County Leader* of Polk and Burnett counties in northwest Wisconsin, had the resources to be able to publish its first edition in 1934 (and still going strong as of today) because they could count on the advertising revenue of the many co-ops that sprung up in these counties from the late 19th century onward. Co-ops for local dairy creameries or the People's Co-Op Oil Association in Luck or the People's Garage in Milltown, were just some of this base of advertisers.

Whether it was a newspaper, a grain elevator, a mill or creamery, or even a general store, co-ops became as central part of community life as the church and the school was. They became cultural centers for new immigrants groups as well. In Minnesota (where by 1940 there were 600 co-op creameries, 150 mutual insurance companies, 270 co-op farmers elevators plus co-op electric utilities and telephone companies) one could find co-ops linked to Swedes in Vasa, or to Danes in Askov.[14] The Finns set -up lots of co-ops in many communities of the Arrowhead region in the northeast part of the state after they had been blacklisted into farming cut-over land for trying to organize unions in the mines of the Iron Range in the early part of the 20th century. As such centers of the community, they became prime recruiting ground for first, the Farmer's Union, and then the political parties the Union formed the base of, the Non-Partisan League, Farm-Labor and Progressives. So much so that the in the early 1920s the Republicans, (led by Minnesota U.S. Sen. Knute Nelson) fearing permanent loss of the farm votes to these independent parties, organized with the Farm Bureau to form bigger, regional co-ops with more producers with iron-clad contracts to dictate high prices. Some of these co-ops, such as Land O'Lakes, are thriving today.[15]

Immigrant's Song

Wandernlust is a German word meaning "joy of traveling" which, translated in to English, is wanderlust. From the 1830s until the 1920s, many in Europe were filled with wanderlust to leave their homes, their families and their nations behind to travel to a brand new land with almost nothing to take with them except for their dreams.

Had there been no wanderlust, then Wisconsin, by 1860, would not have had a population that was 36 percent foreign born nor Minnesota have a population that was 34 percent.[16] Wisconsin would not have, by 1930, a 50.3 percentage of foreign born residents, of that 41 percent Germans, nor would 75 percent of the strikers in the first major Iron Range work stoppage in Minnesota in 1907 be Finnish.[17] Without wanderlust, there would have been no Volga Germans to break the prairie sod of North Dakota that turned it into the second largest wheat-producing state in the U.S.

Disasters and hardship had come to these peoples of Europe before, war, famine, plague, repression, for thousands of years. If they moved from one area to another at all, it was to another part of the nation or to another part of continent. But by the early 1830s, something had happened to cause the complete abandonment of their homelands for the New World. Something had shaken their respective societies enough to cause the psychological break that allowed them to gather their meager belongings, head for the nearest port and sail away.

War and militarism had something to do with it. German-speaking areas of Europe had been the crossroads of so many battles from 1600 to 1815 that one could hardly keep track. When armies moved through the small villages and towns of central Europe, particularly the *en masse* armies of the Louis XIV and Napoleonic eras, they plundered and confiscated everything they could get their hands on to keep themselves fed and clothed, no questions asked. [18] If you were unlucky enough to be conscripted or kidnapped from your home into serving into one of the mercenary armies of the small German principalities and kingdoms of the Rhine River (the Hessians of the American Revolutionary period) you were no better than a slave and were treated brutally by your officers to instill harsh discipline in order to fight. It was ironic that the World War I propagandists here in the United States like Committee of Public Information, or in Great Britain pictured the Germans as vicious as the medieval Huns and born to the sword militarists because most Germans immigrants in the United States had left their homeland to avoid military service altogether, especially with the rise of nation-state's massive armed forces like Prussia, Austria-Hungary and Russia. Other immigrants groups that settled in the Upper Midwest also did the same such as the Finns, *Volksdeutschen*, Poles, Czechs and south Slavs. One could slander and smear the German-speaking people of the U.S. as traitors for not supporting World War I, but the reality was they did not like war nor militarism nor conscription period given their history and background and voted this way. It is also why this region, with the exception of North Dakota with its missile silos and Air Force bases, has very few military installations outside of National Guard camps. Any candidate or political party that presented itself as anti-war, or a critic of U.S. foreign policy and or militarism, could expect to get quite a bit of support. A fact that's still true to a certain extent in the Upper Midwest today. [19]

Economics certainly had something to do with immigration. Alongside the political upheaval of war came the economic and social upheaval of the Industrial Revolution. As Europe emerged from feudalism with the rise of the nation-state after the French Revolution, farmers found themselves with little plots of land to feed growing families, much less a whole nation-state. This was particularly true in both Germany and Scandinavia. Tradition called for a father's sons to divide his land upon his death among themselves, but such small scale farming made that impossible. Taking this into account, along with new technologies and machines to improve farm yields and state enforced reforms in the agricultural sector to feed the new nation-state and its conscripted armies, the end result was hundred of thousands of landless peasants.[20] They had to go somewhere. Many flocked to cities to take up work in the burgeoning industries, but others went to America in search of land to continue farming. Rural conservatives from Scandinavia to Germany made this radical decision to preserve a way of life. Of course crops failures helped speed the process along too, famine in Sweden in the 1850s and in the Volksdeutchen farming regions of southern Russia near the Volga and the Black Sea in 1890s, led to the exodus of those immigrant groups. The same happened to tradesmen and skilled craftsmen as well. Once machines did their work a hundred times faster with more products made, they began their exodus too.

And immigration followed the land. Norwegians from the interior of the part of the country, once they had heard by world of mouth about all the available land in American (especially after the Homestead Act was passed in 1862), began their trek to the coastal ports of Trondeim and Bergen and set sail in schooners across the North Sea into the Atlantic. From New York, Boston or Halifax, they made their way west to the land. Their first stop would have been at the Kendall Settlement outside of Rochester, NY., the first large Norwegian settlement in the U.S. Then it was on to open land in Missouri, Indiana, northeastern Iowa, northern Illinois and southern Wisconsin, with a few staying behind to live in Chicago. When these settlements filled, they sought more land in western Wisconsin and Minnesota, following the great northern railroads to the Dakotas, Montana until their final stop in Washington. It's estimated that 87 percent of Norwegian immigrants came this way, searching for land from 1826 to 1910.[21] No nation gave a larger proportion of her people to America, with the exception of Ireland, than Norway. Farming wasn't their only trade, as many Norwegians arrived in the Upper Midwest just in time to join fellow Scandinavians for the great lumber boom of the 1850s through the 1900s.

Immigrants now filled the farmlands and forests, towns and cities of Wisconsin, Minnesota and North Dakota. Parties and candidates looking for votes in the Upper Midwest had to take their interests along with their culture into account especially in Wisconsin, which gave foreign-born residents the right to vote after only one year's residency.

Society was the final part installed into the immigration machine. The year 1815 may have been the end of the Napoleonic Wars, but the Jacobin ideas of *liberte, égalité and fraternité* that the French armies carried with them throughout Europe endured. This sparked political upheaval throughout the continent that spread into America.

Religion began to be affected as liberal and enlightenment movements such as Haugenism in Norway, [22] the free church and Baptist movements in Sweden, the Grundvig movement in Denmark and the turn towards the national Lutheran church (along with the growth of secular nationalist and socialistic internationalist movements) in the wake of Russification in Finland, began to flourish in the 1830s. Such movements challenged the orthodoxy of the state Lutheran churches, broke down old customs and led to detachment from traditional societies. These movements were strong in the rural areas of these countries where most immigrants came from and they were also popular with the young, who were more likely to uproot themselves from their homelands than the old. Such faiths also led to political change as well and worked hand in hand. Norway became an autonomous region of Sweden in 1814 (it became a separate kingdom in 1905) with the signing of the Eidsvold or constitution on the 17th of May (the Syttende Mai still celebrated today in ethnic Norwegian areas of the Upper Midwest.). Parliamentary elections in Norway began in 1837 and political liberalization followed across Scandinavia.[23] Laws ending state persecution of Haugen churches were passed in Norway by the 1840s. From these churches came the ideas that formed the basis for liberal and social democratic political groups that found success later in the 19th and early 20th century.

In central Europe, small Protestant sects such as the Anabaptists, Brethren, Amish, Mennonites and Dunkards, who's pacifism reflected the growing revulsion to war and militarism there, left for America as soon as they could to escape persecution.[24] But secular faiths, such as liberalism, nationalism and socialism began to grow among those in Germany and Scandinavia who were tired of religious influence in politics, tired of foreign domination, and tired of the authoritarian and confiscating rule of kings, emperors and princes who ruled the land before a united Germany. Such liberals, free thinkers and socialists were the brains behind the civil conflicts in 1848, the Year of Revolutions. The Prussian, Austrian and Russian state armies and local *gendarmese* crushed their revolts and forced many who supported them to leave for the United States. Yet their defeat did not dim their views and the German "48ers" became a political base that would go to have much influence both in the Upper Midwest and nationally.[25]

As nation-states began to form, compulsory education began to follow. First Prussia, then a united Germany began to set up public schools to teaching reading and writing for its citizens to function in the liberal age of science, industry and management. Scandinavian nations compelled their churches to provide education to their parishioners. Even as immigrants began to leave throughout the 1800s, they left both educated and open to or at least familiar with the ideas of liberalism and socialism. It would be wrong to say, as former University of Minnesota political science professor Hy Berman put it "that Finns, (for example) carried socialism with them to America in their baggage." [26] Socialism, as movement in Finland, did not have significant strength until 1899 and the Social Democratic party in Sweden did not come to power until 1932. What it did mean, however, is that the candidates who spoke to immigrant enclaves in the Upper Midwest and called for a state owned grain elevator and a moratorium on farm foreclosures, or who called for an eight-hour work day and the right for workers to organize a union, would not be offering ideas that were alien to the immigrants' thinking or their faiths as they would be perhaps in New England or the South with their different cultural and ethnic backgrounds. In fact, they may very well support such ideas and such candidates that promoted them.

Nearer my God to Thee

Religion has been a part of U.S. political parties and factions since the days of the Revolution when high Anglicans stayed loyal to the crown while low Anglicans, Congregationalists and Baptists supported the patriot cause.[27] So it was true among the immigrant farmers of the Upper Midwest. Catholics supported the Democratic Party because it was the only party that would have them. That bond was cemented as early as 1856 when the party platform of that presidential election year condemned the anti-Catholic, anti-immigrant "Know-Nothing" movement of the America Party. In the Upper Midwest, Catholicism was the only base the Democrats had. The party was not referred to, as one Wisconsin pol put it, as "a Polish-Irish marching society" for nothing. Its base in Wisconsin for example, lay with Catholic ethnic groups. Such groups were particularly numerous in the eastern counties of Jefferson, Dodge, Fond du Lac, Sheboygan, Washington, Kewaunee, Shawano, and Manitowoc. Some of the populations of these counties were over 60 percent German Catholic joined by Dutch, French, Polish, Irish and Belgian Catholics as well.[28] Thus it was no surprise that Democratic Governor William Taylor received 60 percent of the vote in several of these same counties in the election of 1873. The same was true in Minnesota as counties such as Stearns, Brown, and Winona (which are home to the Catholic dioceses of St. Cloud, New Ulm and Winona respectively) were heavily German Catholic (numerous Polish Catholics in Winona as well) to go along with Irish Catholics in St. Paul as the Democratic base.[29] The Democrats also had support in Irish quarters of North Dakota and among the Catholic *Volksdeutschen*.

Since the Democrats were the party "Romanism" along with "rum and rebellion," Protestants naturally supported the Republicans whether they were the Methodist, Presbyterian, Congregationalist, Episcopalian or Baptist settlers from New England and Upstate New York who were influenced by the Second Great Awakening of 1820-1850, or the subsequent German Lutherans and Calvinists, or Scandinavian state Lutheran or rival free church Lutheran sects and Baptists. One also cannot forget Protestant Celtic groups such as the Scots, Welsh and the Cornish that settled in Wisconsin and Minnesota were also overwhelmingly for the GOP. Such groups opposed slavery, which put them on the side of the United States during the War Between the States, and opposed the liquor trade, which put them in favor of Prohibition. Thus it was not a coincidence that the author of the 18th Amendment, Minnesota Congressman Andrew Volstead, was the son of Norwegian immigrants and represented the heavily Norwegian-settled Red River Valley in his Seventh Congressional District. That's three strikes against the party of "rum, Romanism and rebellion." In the election of 1860, both Wisconsin and Minnesota were in the top 10 of GOP voting states, Minnesota at 63.9 percent and Wisconsin at 58 percent.[30]

Since the three independent political parties of the Upper Midwest were either offshoots of the GOP (Progressive), trying to use the GOP label to their advantage (Non-Partisan League) or trying for parity with the GOP (Farm-Labor), they largely went after the same Republican bases at first. But by the time of the Great Depression, these parties were reaching out to Catholics as well. Since almost everyone suffered from the effects of the great economic downturn of the 1930s, such religious distinctions began to be less important. So there was no reluctance for Phil LaFollette, whose family was descendant from French Protestant Huguenots, to campaign in Eastern Wisconsin or Farm-Labor activists to try and organize in Stearns County.

Plus, a change had come in the Catholic community of the United States. Since the World War I and since New York Governor Al Smith became the first Catholic ever to receive a major party nomination for president, Catholic self-confidence was growing. In the past, Catholic lay groups and priests would not get involved in politics directly or speak out on issues largely in fear of a Protestant and nativist backlash. Now many priests were speaking out at the economic misery around them - armed with the *Rerum Novarum* of Pope Leo XIII, which spelled out the rights and duties of both capital and labor and borrowed heavily on social teachings of St. Thomas Aquinas - along with helping to enroll Catholics in mining towns and big cities into labor unions.[31] This is how Fr. Charles Coughlin began his public career, speaking out against injustices of capitalism and the tyranny of communism to a national audience on the radio. Locally, a priest named Fr. Phillip Gordon, a part-Indian, Vatican educated pastor for St. Patrick's Church in Centuria, Wisconsin in the Progressive stronghold of Polk County, drew crowds anywhere from two to three thousand people for picnics in the early 1930s to benefit local farmers where he would speak in their favor and invite local politicians to take part. The Farm-Labor party reached out to Catholics by gathering support from the Catholic Italian, Slavic and Irish miners on the Iron Range while North Dakota Congressman and Non-Partisan League member William Lemke, a Protestant, was tapped by Coughlin to head the ticket as the presidential candidate for the Coughlin-founded Union Party. Another Minnesotan, Monsignor John A. Ryan, helped to write the 1919 U.S. Bishop's Program for Social Reconstruction that endorsed unemployment and old age insurance, public housing and a tax on excess profits.[32]

Catholicism and Protestantism were the main religions of the Upper Midwest but one cannot overlook Jewish influences as well despite their small numbers. The north side of Minneapolis was a solid neighborhood of Jewish immigrants from Europe and Minnesota's first Farm-Labor governor, Floyd B. Olson, made many friends while growing up there, some of whom became his advisors or were appointed to head state agencies. Jewish immigrants in Milwaukee also played a role in the strong Socialist Party there which ran the city from 1910-1960. [33]

Choosing sides

Economics, ethnicity and religion were a few of the ways voters were broken down into respective parties and political groups. There were other issues as well that made voters choose sides.

The War Between the States created divisions within the U.S. body politic that lasted for at least 100 years. The Upper Midwest identified with the Union side and subsequently, the Republican Party. That loyalty was sealed with blood of the Iron Brigade from Wisconsin, the Old Abe war eagle, Arthur

McArthur's famed "On Wisconsin!" battle cry at Missionary Ridge, or the doomed charge of 1st Minnesota at Gettysburg. It was also sealed with ethnic faces as well. Carl Schurz and Franz Siegel may not have been the best officers in the Northern armies when it came to fighting battles, but they did invaluable work in rallying German immigrants to the Union cause, at least among the Protestants and the 48ers.[34] Siegel was an officer in Baden during the Revolution of 1848 while Schurz was a young adjutant to the commandant of the Rastatt fortress.[35] On the Catholic side, things were different. Not only Germans, but Belgians and Dutch as well resisted the draft, their anti-conscription mindset firmly in place. They were also indifferent to what they saw was a Protestant war, the latest chapter in the struggle between the Puritans and High Anglicans carried over from England to America. Indeed, Pope Pius IX was one of the few foreign leaders to give recognition to the Confederacy. Thus, with a noticeable lack of volunteers, Wisconsin needed a draft quota for the army by 1862 which was resisted by riots in the Catholic belt of Brown, Kewaunee, Washington, Milwaukee and Ozaukee counties in the eastern part of the state. Rioters in Port Washington, the Ozaukee County seat, stormed the courthouse, seized and destroyed draft enrollment records and beat Union-supporting county officials. [36]

On the other side of the state, there were no draft riots. Norwegians proclaimed their loyalty to the North in the person of Gen. Hans Christian Heg, the son of settlers in the first Norwegian village in Wisconsin at Muskego. He died in the battle of Chickamauga and was lionized after his death to bind Norwegians and other Scandinavians to the Union and the Republican Party, so much so that his statue stands at the east entrance of state capital in Madison. Swedish immigrant John Ericsson did his bit for the Union war effort by designing the Monitor which saved the U.S. fleet from destruction by the *CSS Virginia* in the battle of Hampton Roads.[37]

Given the percentages of foreign born in the Upper Midwest, the Republicans quickly dropped nativism as a potential selling point of their party, even though it was in the roots of their New England wing and their fellow travelers who settled the Midwest in her name. Early Republicans started out competing for votes with the American Party in 1856 on the issue of anti-immigration. But by 1860 even Abraham Lincoln had bought an interest in a German-language newspaper in Illinois, knowing full well he needed immigrant votes to win the Midwest.[38] Still, German support for the war by the time of Lincoln's re-election 1864 declined in many German-centric counties like Stearns in Minnesota. Stearns County has kept that tradition of voting against "war presidents," in higher numbers that before the war whether it was Wilson or Roosevelt and so forth. German-speaking counties also voted against incumbent presidents during even rumors of war. McIntosh County in southern North Dakota, center of the *Volksdeutschen* immigrants, had the sharpest swing against Franklin Roosevelt from the elections 1936 to 1940, 48 points! [39]

Germans in the Upper Midwest were never united around one political party or platform. But they could come together when their interests were threatened. The 1890 gubernatorial election in Wisconsin hinged on a proposal for English-only instruction in the state's public schools. German voters fell behind the Democrat, George Wilbur Peck, later to be renowned as the author of the "Peck's Bad Boy" short story series, and upset the incumbent Republican governor William Dempster Hoard 160,388 votes to 132,068. [40] Some accused Robert "Fighting Bob" LaFollete's opposition to World War I tainted by the state's German population (a slander used against any ant-war politician from a German-speaking area). It was true that LaFollete was loath to risk antagonizing such a large voting bloc, only reluctantly supporting Prohibition by 1916. But his anti-war sentiment was rooted in principals that went beyond ethnic voting blocs. Even so, German voters never forgot his stand against the war and the abuse he took for it along with abuse they took from a nation seized hateful passions caused by the war. They rewarded himself and his sons in later years. North Dakota's NPL also took an antiwar stand that proved beneficial to its efforts among the *Volksdeutschen*.

With the different voting blocs of the Upper Midwest having been planted and grown in the 1800s, economically, ethnically and socially, the Progressives, Farm-Labor and NPL political parties could now harvest them just as the major parties had done before, sometimes with bigger yields.

Chapter 3—The Non-Partisan League

Die Erste hat den Todt. Der Zweite hat die Not und der Dritte erst hat Brot.[1]

Translated from German, this little saying sums up perhaps the entirety of the *Volksdeutschen* experience in North Dakota and maybe perhaps all immigrants in general.

"For the first generation, death. For the second, want and for the third, bread."

That it took so long, 42 years, for the children and grandchildren of the *Volksdeutschen* to finally break bread was something they had already known. It took that long and sometimes even longer for their descendents living in southern Russia along the Black Sea and the Volga River to have bread. Breaking the virgin grasslands of the Peace Garden State with the plow, as their ancestors did on the steppe, was hard, laborious work with plenty of obstacles in the way from the weather, to crop failures, to hunger and disease to marauders, both human and animal. Sacrificing for the future was a way of life for them as it was for many North Dakotans for the first 50 years of statehood.

And part of securing that future had more to do than just

success with the plow. To build the kind of communities the *Volksdeutschen* had in the southern North Dakota, as well the other immigrants and settlers of this prairie frontier, required both faith in God and also an organization that would look after their interests as well and allow them to unite against a common foe even when so much divided them.

For three generations the Non-Partisan League was that organization. For hundreds and thousands of farmers and rural residents, *Volksdeutschen*, Norwegians, Canadians and other ethnic groups as well, the NPL would ensure bread when the process was all through and by 1957, 42 years after its founding, the NPL had done its job. Success often was the NPL's own worst enemy and ultimately led to its eventual demise. But not before helping to shape the North Dakota that we see today and provide the potential for new and different independent political activism in the future, as it seemed to do when founder A.C. Townley dreamed up the NPL to solve the Socialist quandary.

Townley and the Socialist Question

Arthur C. Townley was, at one time, one of the biggest flax farmers in the United States. A native of Minnesota, Townley had 8,000 acres of land in North Dakota under cultivation by 1912 and earned $100,000 a year.[2] Alas, a drought, frost and a sudden drop in prices to under a dollar per bushel put Townley into bankruptcy. Needless to say such a reversal of fortune, with his income now at $50,000 in the red, turned Townley red himself. He became a socialist and threw himself into Socialist Party activism across the state.[3]

But by 1915, few people were buying the SP's message in North Dakota outside of parts of Fargo, the state's largest city, which left Townley frustrated. Traveling across the state for two years, he saw farmers just like himself hurting from deflationary prices. He felt their anger at the high prices railroads charged to ship their grain. He sensed their fury at the local banks, owned by financial chains based out of the Twin Cities of Minneapolis and St. Paul, pressuring farmers to pay their debts or be foreclosed. They wanted the same things the Socialist Party wanted, a state owned grain elevator and bank and protection from predatory railroad shippers. Why wouldn't they join up then?

grain elevator and storage facilties in Wyndmere, North Dakota

Maybe it was due to the fact that the SP only saw voters through the dimension of their labor or class status and didn't realize that man was more complex than that in his thinking and in his identity. Perhaps the SP's ambivalence to downright hostility towards religion wasn't playing well in a society where the church was the only thing tying together diverse communities across the vast prairies. Certainly the SP's ties to radical, industrial labor unions in a state with little industry wasn't helping recruiting efforts and the reputation such unions had for labor strife, strikes and violence could have been dirtying the party's image in the voter's eyes. Not to mention the constant party infighting over theory, strategy and tactics. Of course, trying to make it as a non-major party in a state where the

Republicans were all dominant was going to be tough going no matter what SP believed in or what its image was with the voters.

In the movie *Northern Lights*, the character of Ray Sorenson, a Norwegian farmer living with his family in the northwest part of North Dakota, tells a Socialist store owner in the town of Crosby as they debate the issues: "I've never seen a successful Socialist." [4] Ray was in town campaigning for a new political group, one Townely formed to try and solve the Socialist question: Could a political party advocate what the Socialists were calling for without actually being a Socialist? Could one adopt the ideology without the owning baggage of the political party designed to carry out that ideology? Certainly if in this day and age one can be a libertarian without having anything to do with the Libertarian Party, then Townley and his organizers, who felt just as frustrated as he did with the SP's lack of support in the state, could do the same a century ago. It's just a simple matter of switching from a capital letter to a lower case letter. And just as some libertarians today, through the Republican Liberty Caucus, use the Republican Party label to help promote their views, so too did Townley plan to use the GOP for the same purpose or, as it was best put, "get off the Socialist line and begin speaking an idiom their particular people could cheer."

A red glow on the Northern horizon

One socialist writer described the success of the Non-Partisan League as a "red glow on the Northern horizon."[5] Certainly that was true when it came to the socialist agenda of a state-owned grain elevator and bank and regulation of railroads. But the NPL organized itself along traditional U.S. political lines in clear rejection of socialist models and theories. The NPL built itself a grassroots and populist machine of small farmers, especially in the Norwegian and other Scandinavian settled areas of the state, which could rival any urban political organization in the country.

Townley and his partner William Lemke, the son of a Prussian army officer,[6] sent out their organizing teams in 1915 and 1916 for the new organization. For $6 a person could join and have a personal stake in what technically was a partisan organization, since the NPL would have a direct effect on who won the Republican nomination (the Democrats were as small and impotent here as in the rest of the Upper Midwest but their party nomination could be useful to either the NPL or its opponents to oppose each other in the fall elections). North Dakota's spring open primary, in place since 1915, and the lack of party registration (perhaps there was no need because everyone was assumed to be a Republican anyway) gave the NPL their opening to run candidates in Republican primaries even though they gave little thought or time to the local Republican organizations at all.

On top of this structure, there were issues running in the NPL's favor. Farmers were at the point of desperation while being squeezed in the vise of falling prices and high shipping rates. A 1914 advisory referendum calling for a state-owned grain mill, passed by an overwhelming majority of the voters, was never approved by the legislature.[7] Such desperation led to anger at their perceived enemies and the NPL played this sentiment like a grand piano.

"It was definitely an anti-big city party," David Danbom, political science professor at North Dakota State University, said. "It was anti-Fargo, which was the center of banking in this state. They were against the big millers in the Twin Cities, like Pillsbury and General Mills, which they felt were ripping them off on the true price of their grain. The NPL picked up on that and their attacks on these three cities resonated with the voters. And if the immigrants were largely outsiders in their new lands, they readily identified with a party that was made up of outsiders like them."

The further west you went in North Dakota, the stronger the NPL was.

"To the small farmer, the Twin Cities was the evil empire," Lloyd Omdahl, a former state tax commissioner and lieutenant governor along with being a political science professor at the University of North Dakota said. "They felt exploited by the granaries along with the banks, which had chains all throughout the state, and the railroads, which charged them high shipping rates and wouldn't ship grain from co-op owned grain elevators. And the Twin Cities was the place where these exploiters lived."

Indeed they did. The mansions and other beautiful homes on Summit Ave. in St. Paul were built by the captains of those industries while the farmers of North Dakota felt bitter about living in their simple homes out on the plains. "The toilers or the spoilers, who shall be the masters?" was the NPL's campaign message in the spring of 1916 as articulated by Townley.[8] And it was a message powerful enough to sweep the NPL to victory. The head of the ticket, Lynn Fraizer, a farmer, teacher, school board member and township chairman in Pembina County, was elected governor. Bill Langer was elected as state Attorney General and John Baer, a cartoonist for the League's official newspaper who became perhaps the first editorial cartoonist to be elected to public office, was voted into Congress. NPL backed candidates also won enough seats to control the state House of Representatives. Two years later they won control of the State Senate and by 1919-1920 the entire machinery of the state government was in NPL's hands.

The League succeeded, once in power, to enact their socialist agenda without the unpopular Socialist label. Some of that still endures such as the state owned Bank of North Dakota, a state owned grain mill and elevator and statewide income and inheritance taxes. But they became more than just a political organization, much more. By 1918, over 40,000 North Dakotans were registered members of the NPL. Such large numbers and influence allowed it to get involved in banking, publishing and distributing consumer goods to general stores all over the state. Meanwhile, Townley traveled to several nearby states in the Midwest and West to organize more NPLs. By 1918, Townley had signed up 188,365 members and famous politicians like Charles Lindberg Sr. of Minnesota and Sen. Burton K. Wheeler of Montana ran on the NPL line in their respective states. [9]

But the power the NPL accumulated ultimately led to its eventual downfall. Splits began to form within the NPL leadership between Townley and Langer. Factions began to form around each strong-willed man, particularly as Langer, as state attorney general, began to investigate several NPL leaders for corruption. Langer later broke with the League and attacked it, summing up the feeling that the League had become what it was set-up to oppose, a corporation. That sense was also felt by the state's network of farmer-owned co-ops which were instrumental in helping to organize the League, but now saw it as a competitor in the marketplace. On top of that, an agricultural depression in prices after the First World War, coupled with another drought in the western part of the state, forced the state bank to foreclose on the very farmers it was supposed to serve. The war itself hurt the NPL as many accused it of being unpatriotic, pro-German and pro-communist for not fully supporting or being very enthusiastic about the war. Plus, an opposition to the NPL began to form in 1918 as the Independent Voters Association (IVA) organized and challenged them in GOP primaries. Although the NPL ticket of Fraizer and Lemke as attorney general won again in 1920, they didn't stay in office for long. That same year, Frazier signed into law a bill that allowed for the recall of elected officials, a mainstay of progressive governmental reform. In 1921, the IVA organized just such a recall against Frazier, Lemke and state agriculture commissioner John Hagen. Not for any malfeasance mind you, but the same gross mismanagement charge used against former California governor Gray Davis during his recall election of 2003, despite the fact that such problems did not prevent them from being re-elected several months earlier. Nevertheless, on Oct. 21, 1921, all three men were successfully recalled and the NPL found itself out of power. [10]

Just as the NPL was losing power in 1921 in North Dakota, so did the drive to form NPL-like organizations in other states lose its power as well. Townley had pretty much dropped out of League organizing activities by that same year, moving on to other ventures such as the National Producers Alliance, speculating in oil, and running for office or trying to influence the political scene in Minnesota and North Dakota throughout the 1930s to the 1950s until his death in 1959.[11] Other NPL chapters in other states either withered on the vine or merged with other groups as they did in Minnesota to form the Farm-Labor Party. But in North Dakota, especially with the election Fraizer to the Senate in 1922, the NPL stayed alive and well as they battled the IVA for control of the state throughout the 1920s, rendering the major political parties all but pawns in their grand chess game. The League would again emerge as major political force, not just in the state but nationally as well, a decade later formed around several strong personalities with the help of one particular group.

Ticket splitting

When building coalitions of different voting blocs, political parties and organizations often find it helpful to have their election slate or ticket made up of representatives of each bloc. Each ticket has to be balanced between the different blocs or one of the blocs will not vote for that party if it perceives it's being ignored. Thus, when Allard K. Lowenstein, the famed student activist and Congressman from New York wanted to run for the U.S. Senate in 1974 on the Democratic ticket, he was bluntly told by labor leader Victor Gottbaum that "Allard, when are you going to get it through your thick skull? I need another Jew on this ticket like I need another asshole!"[12]

The same was true for the Non-Partisan League as they balanced Norwegian, old Yankee, Slavic, Canadian and *Volksdeutschen* interests with their election slates. And William Langer was right in the middle of it. Along with William Lemke, they were the NPL's liaison with the Volksdeutchen. Ever since Lemke won his first race for political office, as Morton County District Attorney in 1914 by handing out German language pamphlets, speaking fluent German was a big asset for both Langer's career and the NPL's. [13]

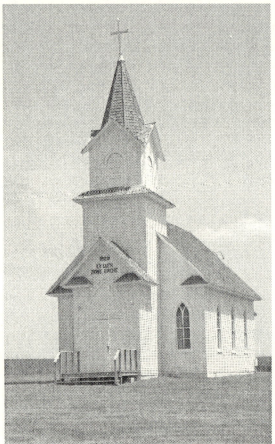

A *Volksdeutschen* church located outside Ashley, North Dakota

The NPL's radical agenda sold well to Norwegians and other Scandinavian farmers familiar with such thinking, but getting the *Volksdeutschen* to go along was difficult because such ideas were not a part of their tight-knit communities. When the *Volksdeutschen*, literally the Germans living outside of Germany proper unlike their opposites the *Reichsdeutschen*, settled in the Russian Empire at the invitation of Czarina Catherine the Great in 1763, they were promised free land, freedom of religion, local self-government and exemption from military service.[14] Such benefits of settlement hardly made them receptive to calls from the socialists and radicals within the empire compared to the peasant serfs or those serfs who, after the Emancipation of 1862 by Czar Alexander II, were free to leave their villages and became part of the great industrial workforce that ultimately led to the Russian Revolution. Since they had already benefited for leaving their homes in Württemberg, Baden, Alsace and the Rhine Palatinate to settle in southern Russia, their main concerns were farming and preserving their culture, religion and themselves in a harsh landscape. Their status-quo and religious based conservatism is a result of that and stayed with them as they came to America. If you want to know where Pat Buchanan did his best in the 2000 presidential election as the Reform Party candidate, check out the counties of McIntosh, Emmons and Logan.[15]

But loyalty to the GOP was another trait as the Republicans' support of the Homestead Act of 1862 helped them purchase their farms quite cheaply on a landscape most familiar to them. They escaped conscription, drought and Russification and were not going to be rebels by nature. Certainly Bill Kretschmar's family wasn't. The son and grandson of local bankers in Ashley, North Dakota, the Kretschmars were pillars of their *Volksdeutschen* community, but also a part of the system that the NPL regarded with such distaste. Ashley, lying within McIntosh County in the southern part of the state, is part of the of what the locals call the "Iron Triangle" and outsiders refer to as the "Sauerkraut Triangle," basically the area of *Volksdeutschen* settlement in the state extending north to Rugby, west to Lemmon and east to Ellendale. Inside are towns such as Wishek, Munich, Berlin, Kulm, Fredonia, Lehr, Strasburg, Napoleon and New Leipzig. By 1920, 23 percent of all *Volksdeutschen* from

Russia lived in North Dakota and by 1997 the region still had 75 percent of its residents claim German ancestry.[16]

"How well you do among the Russian-German population was an important part of carrying this part of the state and carrying the Iron Triangle," Kretschmar said. "To a certain degree it still is, especially if you are a Republican because McIntosh County is one of the strongest GOP counties in the state."[17]

Having that GOP label was helpful to Langer as it was for Kretschmar. He began to practice law in partnership with his cousin in Ashley in 1961 and from 1972-1998, was a part of the North Dakota state House of Representatives, rising up the ranks to become speaker for a time. Although beaten for re-election in 1998, he won his seat again in 2000 and has been re-elected ever since. Given the state's part time legislature, his law office is still open mornings off of Ashley's Main St., the county seat.

Kretschmar's family was well acquainted with Langer. His grandfather was a state senator from 1910-1918 and again from 1922-1930. His father ran the family's bank, which was based out of another little *Volksdeutschen* community of Venturia. Economic policy was not something that was going to bring Langer and the NPL together with a prominent family like the Kretschmars

"I remember my father telling me one time he and some other bankers from this area met with Langer when he first became governor in 1933," Kretschmar said. "The Depression was pretty severe around here. Prices were bad and we had the drought that led to the dust storms that swept all over the Plains. We called it the 'Dirty 30's.' Anyway, Langer met with local bankers to talk about Langer's plan for a foreclosure moratorium that he campaigned for the year before. These banks were holding all these mortgages that weren't paying anything and Langer was telling them 'Look boys, I've made this promise. Politically I can't change it.'"

Despite their economic differences, Langer was popular

with all layers of the *Volksdeutschen* community and was able to build his NPL organization, "Langer's League" as it was called in the early 1930s, with the help of established, large and prominent families from the community to serve as his precinct captains, loyal to him, from township to township.[18] Two important issues also helped. One was defending the teaching of German in the *Volksdeutschen* schools in 1917 while state Attorney General as the anti-German hysteria let loose by President Woodrow Wilson's declaration of war on Germany started to crank up. The other was opposition to war itself along with many other leading NPL figures.[19] The *Volksdeutschen* never forgot this, especially in light of their own experiences fleeing Russia due to efforts to eliminate the teaching of German there during the Russification policies of Czars Alexander III and Nicholas II. The *Volksdeutschen* may have adopted a few Russian delicacies to their taste pallets like havalah (crushed, sweetened sesame seeds) and some clothes like babushkas and schlapps to their wardrobes, but they always held fast to their German tongues and religions.[20]

Langer got back into politics in 1928, running for attorney general again. He lost by a significant margin as the whole NPL ticket was beaten badly, marking their nadir for the 1920s. But the oncoming Depression gave the NPL another chance as an alternative in voters' minds as Langer was slowly but busily rebuilding the League's apparatus neglected for many years. By 1932, the NPL produced what would be for them a political dream team, the slate of Langer for governor, Lemke for U.S. House and Gerald P. Nye for U.S. Senate. Such a team wouldn't stay local for long.

Taking it national

By 1930, North Dakota had reached its peak population at just over 600,000 residents. Here was one of the smallest states in the Union in terms of population and yet it had three politicians of national reputation.

It was by then that the NPL had made its impact on the national scene, just as Floyd B. Olson had done in Minnesota in 1931-32 with the Farm-Labor Party and just as Robert LaFollette had done earlier with his Progressive Party.

Langer made his mark by, of course, being Langer. His term as governor was a combination of bombastic style, like using the state's National Guard 31 times in 1933 to prevent farm foreclosures; forcing the state mill to buy drought-stricken wheat at fixed prices and embargoing North Dakota wheat from the rest of the country to raise prices, to more concrete results in Depression relief measures he pushed through the legislature early in his term. Of course, the fact the state went through four governors in seven months between 1934 and 1935, after Langer had been forced to step down as a result of being indicted for corruption, also gave the state plenty of unwanted notoriety as well.[21]

But also on the national scene were Sen. Gerald P. Nye and Rep. William Lemke. Both were elected to Congress in 1932 and it didn't take long for either to make an impact.

Nye was first. A newspaperman for much of his adult life, he jumped from the editorial page of the Griggs County Courier-Journal to the U.S. House of Representatives in 1926, and then from there to the Senate. In his first term, he and other Progressive Republicans like Robert LaFollette Jr. of Wisconsin and George Norris of Nebraska were approached by the Women's International League of Peace and Freedom to investigate the international arms and munitions industry. After extensive lobbying of the Senate leadership, Nye was able to help create the Munitions Investigation Committee which quickly bore his name, the Nye Committee. It was Nye who coined the phrase "merchants of death" and received plenty of attention around the country as his critique of the U.S' entry into the war fit in with the revulsion of the public against the conflict along with the anti-capitalism critique of that early New Deal era. the *Inter-County Leader*, the co-op progressive newspaper of northwest Wisconsin, published plenty of findings and other news from the Committee's hearings, which began Sept. 4 of 1934 and lasted until 1936, as did other progressive, liberal and socialist publications.[22]

In that year, William Lemke stepped to the fore. After making a political comeback in 1932 by being elected to the U.S. House of Representatives, he became a noted spokesperson for the plight of drought- stricken and bankrupt farmers, especially in his own state where some 70 percent of its residents were on some form of public assistance. His name was on several bills that offered relief to farmers, monetary inflation and foreclosure holidays and his name too, was spread far in wide in same publications as Nye's. That got him tapped to head the Union Party ticket in 1936.

The Union Party originated primarily with Fr. Charles Coughlin's National Union for Social Justice (NUSJ). The radio priest had a large following around the country and not just among Catholics. Anyone who felt that centralization, whether from big corporations, the New Deal, or even the Soviet Union, was concentrating power in the hands of only the few and a privileged few at that, could buy into what Coughlin was selling. The seemingly radical swing he took, against Herbert Hoover in 1932 to being almost violently against FDR in 1936 (ripping off his clerical collar during one broadcast) is not as far fetched as it might appear nor so radical. It attracted a diverse, some would say in criticism motley, following to his banner: the remnants of former Sen. Huey P. Long's "Every Man a King" movement, which would have been the platform for Long to run on for president before his assassination in 1935, and Francis Townshed's old-age pension movement that eventually became Social Security.[23]

The precipitating events for the formation of the Union Party were partly Long's assassination and partly the marriage of big government and big business in the form of the National Recovery Administration. The NRA's job was to get large businesses to work with (some would say collude was more like it) the government in order to raise prices and standardize production in an effort to fight back against price deflation. Its welter of codes and regulations along with its extreme socialistic overtones, with its blue eagle emblem and Washington-promoted rallies, alarmed many, especially in the Midwest. The NRA's inability to work as advertised along with its aforementioned reputation sparked protest that Coughlin hoped he could take advantage of with a political party. Picking the nominees himself, Coughlin chose the Protestant Lemke and Catholic former Boston prosecutor Thomas C. O'Brien as the president/vice-president of his new party.[24] Picking a Protestant in an age when Catholics at one time could not even speak to them showed how the shared suffering of the Depression had melted old hatreds that would ironically pay dividends for the Democratic Party in the Upper Midwest in the years to come.

Such notoriety for these three North Dakota politicians along with LaFollette and Olson could only have happened through their iconoclasm, their ability to work outside strict party structures on the state or national level and their taking on of important issues with independent political backing. Hack politicians don't make waves and don't step out of line unless told to do so and if they do otherwise, they are punished by the machine or the establishment or whatever the powers that be are called. Men like LaFollette, Olson, Langer, Lemke and Nye were able to strike out on their own because they had political infrastructures to back them up. This allowed them to speak out on issues they cared about or get results, whether through an independent party or through a faction they controlled of a major party.

Olson, like Langer, gained fame as a governor, and they pushed their respective states beyond what the federal government was doing at the time for Depression relief and by taking the initiative and showing leadership among the

Midwest's governors. Olson in particular sponsored such measures as a two-year moratorium on farm foreclosures, old-age pension laws, unemployment insurance, statutes prohibiting court injunctions in labor disputes and personally settled strikes himself. Those accomplishments put him on the fast track with quite a following in the Upper Midwest (with good promotion from the *Inter-County Leader* who's readers live near the Minnesota border in northwest Wisconsin) and nationwide thanks to fawning features in *The New Republic* and *The Nation* and a plug in the book *Puzzled America* by Sherwood Anderson.[25] Historian and former University of Minnesota political science teacher Hy Berman feels Olson, had he not died of cancer in 1936, could have become Roosevelt's vice-president in 1940 and potential successor. While Olson was as radical as Henry Wallace, being an ex-Democrat and in the New Deal party of Minnesota with drawing power enough to take the farm vote away from the Republicans, would have been better help to Roosevelt compared to the former Republican and mystic Wallace, whose own version of the Progressive Party in 1948 ultimately became a Stalinist front. The F-L's success at producing national figures in politics would come much later after its merger with the Democrats.

Neither Phil nor Robert LaFollette Jr. ever enjoyed the kind of national prominence that their famous father once did (although Phil did try to organize a national progressive party after becoming disenchanted with the Roosevelt Administration). Much of their political success rested on the foundation their father built for himself, which included a national reputation for honesty, progressivism and principle for standing up against U.S. entry into World War I. LaFollette first gained that reputation for cleaning up Wisconsin politics as governor, rooting out corruption and breaking the hold the railroads had on the state. When he moved up to the Senate in 1905, he maintained that reputation by being the intellectual and inspirational force behind the move to drive out the autocratic

Speaker of the House Joe Cannon in 1911. A year later he tried to run for president, hoping to use the kind of party primaries that he had helped to set-up in Wisconsin to win the GOP nomination. But Theodore Roosevelt outmuscled LaFollette and took control of progressive politics himself in that year, which then later passed to Woodrow Wilson. LaFollette had his name put in nomination at the Republican Convention of 1916 and ran in the primaries against Calvin Coolidge in 1924, hoping beyond hope to catch fire in a party that didn't take a very high view of him. And of course, being one of only six U.S. Senators to oppose Wilson's Declaration of War in 1917 helped him stand out as well, either as a hero or a sore thumb depending on your point of view.

While his stand on the war was unpopular at the time, LaFollette never wavered from it. "I would not change my record on the war for that of any man, living or dead,"[26] he announced to thunderous applause in a packed Wisconsin State Assembly chamber. Disillusionment from the war and the respect he earned for taking a stand helped to revive his career to the point where he could be considered a serious presidential contender nationally again. And unconstrained by any party affiliation, the first incarnation of the Progressive Party was the movement at its purest: a coalition of labor, farmers, small businessmen, intellectuals, socialists (the Socialist Party endorsed LaFollette and he ran of SP lines in some states), liberal Christians, housewives and just about anyone else dissatisfied with the politics of the 1920s came under the LaFollette banner at its 1924 nominating convention in Cleveland.[27] LaFollette had been moving leftward since the end of the World War I and his platform calling for nationalization of railroads, direct election of federal judges (although conservatives of today sometimes speak in favor of this) free trade, the development of an electric power plant at Muscle Shoals, Alabama (the precursor of the Tennessee Valley Authority) reflected this, but the Progressives were not just a leftwing protest party. [28] They thought they had a real chance of throwing the election into the House of Representatives where a coalition of Democratic and Republican leftists and progressives from independent political parties (which would have included the NPL of North Dakota and Farm-Labor of Minnesota), all elected in 1922 with the help of the Conference for Progressive Political Action (CPPA), could win the election. This group became the foundation of new party. With the GOP going for Coolidge in the shadow of scandals from the Harding administration and the Democrats settling on the conservative Wall Street lawyer John W. Davis as a compromise candidate from its tumultuous convention (nominated on the 103rd ballot!), progressives in both parties would naturally flock to LaFollette's banner, giving him a real shot a winning. Or so the theory went.[29]

Alas, LaFollette's forces found out the hard way, as Theodore Roosevelt did, that progressivism simply could not exist as an independent force outside the two-party system. The campaign lacked funds to get its message out and many groups that could have helped sat on their hands, convinced that Coolidge would win big.[30] LaFollette too, lacked the energy needed to run the kind of national campaign he would need to be a factor, being only a year away from death. LaFollette finished third with 17 percent of the vote and won only one state, his own Wisconsin. Still, he showed how impotent the Democrats were in the north and west by finishing ahead of Davis in 11 states, including Minnesota and North Dakota. Eventually, someone would figure out a way to combine the votes of LaFollette and Davis but that would be eight years into the future. However, the campaign did serve as an important training ground for his sons Robert Jr. and Phil to be able to create a new Progressive Party 10 years later.[31]

Just as the LaFollette for President campaign fizzled, so too did Lemke's. The Union Party was Coughlin's brainchild but neither he nor his ally, former Huey Long associate the Rev. Gerald L.K. Smith, mentioned the one called "Liberty Bill" very much in their campaign speeches. Instead, both spellbinders tried to outdo the other in vitriolic rhetoric that someone like Lemke was simply uncomfortable doing. As a candidate from a rural, Northern state and a Protestant, Lemke was incapable of prying away urban Catholics or rural Southerners from the Democratic Party for he knew nothing of their issues or their backgrounds. Lemke could talk farm issues and play up the inflationary monetary bill that he sponsored, but nothing else.[32] The Union Party tried to bring together all the anti-New Dealers on the left and right who either didn't want to associate with what they felt was a damned and discredited Republican Party or with likewise unpopular parties on the left. The problem was there were simply too many of them to form a coherent ideology and program to compare to the New Deal. Meanwhile, the Republicans and their base of support, while smaller, would not go away. And like the Progressives, Farm-Labor and even the NPL, Roosevelt and the Democrats could simply pick and choose policies like Social Security or change their rhetoric to co-opt and rob such parties of their ideas and issues simply because they could. They were in the majors and the rest were the minors. With support from just two percent of the electorate, the Union Party died quickly after 1936. Still, Lemke's best states were the ones in the Upper Midwest where he polled between five and 13 percent in North Dakota, Minnesota and Wisconsin. With Coughlin's help, he polled 10 percent in predominately Irish and German Catholic precincts across the country.

Lemke's career pretty much came to a close after 1936. The Non-Partisan League would soon follow thereafter.

Just fade away

The 1932 election showed that the NPL was back in force. Langer had built a new coalition around the Farmer's Union and the *Volksdeutschen* to go along with its traditional elements. But the NPL of the 1930s lacked the kind statewide solidarity that it had when it formed in 1915. Langer built the party township by township and precinct by precinct. But he made sure the local leaders were personally loyal to him which pretty soon meant that factions would soon appear again, especially among the talented but also strong-willed men that would form the top of its electoral tickets. It also meant a compressed, stand apart and top-down leadership from Langer that inevitably became autocratic and further split the party. The 30's version of the NPL was constructed very much like any political party of that time. But in so doing, it would soon lose it way and then lose itself.

"There was no middle ground with Bill Langer," Bill Kretschmar said. "You either loved him or you hated him. Even here in southern North Dakota, it was the same way."

This showed itself when Langer was accused by federal officials in 1934, particularly Harry Hopkins, head of the Federal Emergency Relief Administration (FERA) and a close aide to FDR, for trying to force federal employees working on relief projects to contribute monies from their salaries to the NPL's official newspaper. The resulting federal indictment forced Langer out office for three years as he battled the Feds in court, ultimately getting the charges dismissed. In the meantime the party split as Nye, encouraged by Hopkins, called for Langer to be investigated on the Senate floor, angering Langer's supporters and forcing NPL leaders to choose sides. The state's political scene became a comic opera as it went through four governors in a seven month period (including one who was removed because he had violated state residency requirements).[33] Trying to hold onto power, Langer even ran his wife for the governor's office in 1934 (something George Wallace would successfully do himself with his wife Lurleen in 1966). Langer would ultimately regain power in the 1936 election, but he had to do so as an independent as he lost the GOP nomination to the NPL-backed incumbent Walter Welford. This led to a full scale split from NPL as Langer, tired of being harassed by his local enemies, ran for the U.S. Senate against three League icons: Nye in 1938 where he was beaten, Frazier in 1940 where he won the GOP nomination and Lemke (who ran as an independent) in the 1940 general election which he finally won. It took a while for him to be seated as charges of vote fraud were in the air, but ultimately he left the state.[34]

Langer stayed popular from his time in the Senate until his death in 1960. But the party he helped to found was shifting under his feet. Two forces were responsible. One was from the establishment Republican side which, led by future U.S. Senator Milton Young, was working overtime to eliminate the League's influence within the party and make it a less hospitable place for them. The other was from the liberal Farmer's Union which wanted the NPL to ally itself from the Democrats. Years of federal largess to the countryside had created a constituency for federal aide to farmers represented by the Union. Since it was the Democrats and the New Deal that created and nurtured such programs, it was only natural, many thought, that the NPL should be working with the party of Roosevelt. Such thoughts had a great appeal to younger politicians and activists, like Lloyd Omdahl.[35]

"The Farmer's Union was a very prominent part of the Non-Partisan League and they were quite liberal," Omdahl said. "They wanted all the liberals in one tent instead of divided by party and by that time the NPL was failing to gain much in the GOP. They identified with Roosevelt, Truman and the Democrats and that's were they wanted the NPL to go."

And go they did. Pushing aside the old guard, conservative Irish and German Catholic Democrats (just as the Progressives did in Wisconsin and Farm-Labor did in Minnesota) the NPL officially merged with the Dems at a statewide convention in Bismarck in 1955. Actually the term "takeover" would suit the situation better since there wasn't much of Democratic Party in North Dakota outside of patronage federal office holders even after 12 years of Roosevelt and eight of Truman. The NPL could have maintained its independence in choosing its own nominees like it did with the GOP, but what would be the point? Now they had a major party label all to themselves and there was no need to be "non-partisan" anymore. Older NPL members like Langer opposed such changes and stubbornly stayed with the GOP (which was soon joined by old Catholic Democrats now out a party). Yet with Langer's death, the old NPL soon faded away to become nothing more than an antique window dressing to today's Democrats in North Dakota.

"There was a newness to the Democrat Party that appealed to young, especially to those growing up in the Depression or having fought in the war," Kretschmar said. "They were coming into their own and with other young persons changed politics in this state. With older people, they're tougher to change and still pretty conservative, especially those folks from my part of the state."

Pretty soon these new Democrats were starting to win victories. Quinten Burdick, the son of popular NPL Congressman Usher Burdick, won his father's congressional seat in 1958 as a Democrat. By 1960, Burdick moved upon Langer's death to the U.S. Senate and the party controlled the governor's office from 1960-1980. The party lines remain remarkably similar to those set up back in 1955. The GOP is still the dominant party in the state when it comes to presidential politics, local offices and the legislature, but the Democrats dominate Congressional offices and can, with the right candidate and circumstances, elect a governor or other statewide candidates. The fact that the Dems have controlled all of North Dakota's congressional seats since 1987 may come as a shock to red state partisans, but those with an understanding of North Dakota politics know better as the major party lines were drawn years ago and have held to this day.

"Here in North Dakota, people vote Republican for president or local offices because they are seen as the white party," NDSU professor David Danbom said. "But they'll vote for the Democrats for Congress and some local offices to look after their economic interests in Washington or here at home."

Indeed they will, just as the Farmer's Union had planned it by the mid-1950s. The polarization of American politics after World War II along with the homogenization of the culture and the blurring and lessening of ethnic and religious distinctions, at least among whites, contributed to the decline and fall of the NPL. To be a Democrat or a Republican today is more than just a pure cultural identity as it was over 60 years ago, but an identity created by a cultural ideology. Yet the NPL realized the power that such labels, Democrat or Republican, had in those days, which is why its founders eschewed the Socialist Party line and went for the dominant Republicans, bringing their ideology along with them. Their tactic of using that party line to advance their goals is still relevant today as a growing group of independent political activists are beginning to realize.

Chapter 4—The Farm Labor Party

"...It's been quiet week in Lake Woebegone, my home on the prairie."

The opening line to Garrison Keillor's monologue that has made him perhaps one of the most famous Minnesotans in the last three decades, leads the listeners of his popular public radio show *A Prairie Home Companion* to a part of the state that's always referred to as "Greater," although economics doesn't always bare that out. One can find "Norwegian bachelor farmers" in places like Lake Woebegone (although where Keillor originally grew up, Anoka, the prairies have been or are in the process of being bulldozed to build Twin Cities subdivisions) and one can find Lake Woebegones in an area that forms an "L" from the Canadian border to the Mississippi River. The vertical line of the L was settled primarily by Norwegians and is rich in wheat and sugar beets, but still retains some of its prairie characteristics as you head towards the Dakotas. The horizontal part of the L was settled mostly by Germans and is much an extension of Iowa as it heads north all the way to the Minnesota River and the southern edge of the Twin Cities, filled mostly with corn, hogs and other row crops.[3]

That's the farm part.

Going back to the Twin Cities themselves, Minneapolis and St. Paul, one used to see the industries set up to service these farms, the great millers and stackers of wheat named Pillsbury, Crosby and Washburn, or the great tractor factory Minneapolis-Moline, or the central hub for the great northern railroads as a place for hogs and other farm animals to congregate. Big rivers begat commerce and the Mississippi and all the business that it brought made the Twin Cities and then its subsequent suburbs and exurbs eventually possible by the laborers that filled them in. Go even further to the north and east, in an area once populated exclusively by trees, wolves, bears, moose and Indians, and one finds it populated with laborers who wouldn't have gone to this wild place had not been for the discovery of the element that made the 19th and 20th centuries work, iron, before it was replaced by another element that was later seen as the world's salvation, silicon.

That's the labor part.

A barn is one of the tallest structures found on the prairies and fields of western Minnesota near Breckenridge

Since 1896, when Williams Jennings Bryan first ran for president, populists, reformers, leftists, socialists and any sort of malcontent or crusader wondered how one could unite the peoples of town and country, farm and factory under a single political banner. Bryan tried three times and failed and Woodrow Wilson had some success but it didn't last long. The personal touch that was needed to bring together city slickers and hayseeds into one powerful political coalition was not lost upon a certain Floyd B. Olson, whom, with his associates, built an impressive non-major party organization than ran the state for much of the 1930s and ultimately put together one of the most powerful state Democratic parties in the country. One that served as mirror on the party as whole before tract homes, recessions, demographics, taxes and ultimately culture conspired together by fate to kill it and what it stood for.

Putting two and two together

A farmer is just as much a working man as a factory worker or a miner, but his views towards his labor are going to be in a different prism. That's because a farmer owns land and pays taxes on it, no matter how small the plot. Holding onto that land and making a profit from it to provide for and pass on to his family is his primary concern and affects the politics the farmer has. He can be a radical if ownership of his land is at stake and be quite conservative in order to use that land as he or (in some cases) she sees fit in order to make it work. Before World War II, a laborer didn't own much more than his or her labor power. A laborer can be conservative if that labor is perceived at stake; meaning not having any at all and watching his or her family starve. Or he or she may turn radical if working conditions are so tough; they have nothing left to lose.

Thus the dilemma for leftists, reformers, socialists, progressives or anyone else who wanted to unite such forces, for neither farmer nor laborer was either one thing or the other at the same time until the Great Depression when all suffered. Laborers didn't respond too well to Bryan's campaigns nor did farmers flock to the banner of the more urban socialists, or progressive Democratic presidential nominees like James M. Cox in 1920 and especially Al Smith in 1928.

If they ever could get together they might find a responsive audience in Minnesota. The official designation may be The North Star State but, as former University of Minnesota political science professor Hy Berman points out, it could easily be called The Maverick State.[2] Going all the way back to Republican-turned-Populist orator Ignatius Donnelly in the late 19th century, mavericks get a long look and a warm smile from Minnesota voters and the lack of a strong two-party system in the state allowed for their fruition. The roll call is formidable: Donnelly, John A. Johnson (one of the few Democrats elected governor before 1954 with the help of a coalition of populists and progressive Republicans), Charles Lindbergh Sr., Elmer C. Benson, Harold Stassen, Cora Knudtsen (of "Cora, Come Home" fame) Hubert Humphrey (in his early career), Eugene McCarthy, Paul Wellstone and the one and only Jesse "The Body," Ventura. This was also a good state for such presidential candidates like Robert LaFollette, Henry Wallace and Ross Perot.[3]

"This state does have a place in its heart for center or center-left independent political movements," *Minneapolis Star-Tribune* political reporter Dane Smith said. "It goes back throughout our history from the moralistic New England settlers, to the Scandinavians and the socialist and progressive influences along with prairie populism. The 'little fellers vs. Rockerfellers' aspect that Paul Wellstone used to talk about is part of our psyche and it's out there for anyone to tap into." [4]

But how, especially as labor developed into its own political orbit? Unlike North Dakota, Minnesota had a significant industrial workforce. Unlike Wisconsin, that workforce was politically active. Unionization without employer retaliation didn't take off in Wisconsin until the 1930s. What unions there were supported the Socialists, especially in Milwaukee given the concentration of the state's heavy industry there. [5] Plus, many Wisconsin industrialists like Walter Kohler of the Kohler bathroom fixtures company, Harry Bradley of the Allen-Bradley company, Jerome I. Case of J.I. Case farm and construction machinery, William Harley and Arthur Davidson of Harley-Davidson motorcycle fame, the Allis-Chalmers tractor works and the great brewing families of Milwaukee like Schlitz, Pabst and Miller, were corporate paternalists who, in some cases, built whole towns (like Kohler and West Allis) around their factories and took care of their workers with their own pension plans, profit sharing, heath insurance and the like to keep away pesky union organizers for as long as they could until they were dragged kicking and screaming into it. [6] Wisconsin had iron mines on the Gogebic Range with radical socialist, communist and syndicalist Finns living along Lake Superior's southern shore close by. But nowhere near what there were in numbers on the great Iron Range.[7]

So whether it was meatpackers in southern Minnesota towns like Austin or Albert Lea; mill workers, brewery workers, factory workers, railroad engineers or truck drivers in the Twin Cities; or miners on the Range, there was a base of labor union members that could be turned into political activists and reliable voters. [8] Original Minnesota reform movements focused on agriculture and the educated, upper middle classes. The labor movement came into its own politically with the election of Socialist Thomas Van Lear as mayor of Minneapolis in 1916 and demanded its say when it came to politics. Voters on the Range voted for a party called Union Labor.

Just about the same time, the Non-Partisan League began to form in the state. Native Minnesotan Arthur C. Townley came back home from North Dakota in triumph in the summer of 1916 after watching his NPL slate clean house in the spring Republican primary, which all but assured their election in the fall. He moved the League's national headquarters to St. Paul in 1917.[9] Now he would replicate the same success here, forming the NPL as the successor to the Grange, Greenback and Populist movements to take on the entrenched interests in the belly of the beast in farmers' minds. And there were plenty of "beasts." The great millers of Minneapolis, Van Dusen-Harrington, Heffelfinger, Pillsbury, Crosby, Washburn and Croke, were in charge. They dominated the local chamber of commerce, who were referred to as the "Sacred 550," and they dominated the local grain exchange markets through 75 commodities trading firms linked to them. Those facts, coupled with the struggles Minnesota wheat, dairy, corn and sugar beet farmers had with low prices, high shipping rates and high interest rates charged by local banks just as in North Dakota, stoked rural anger.[10] The NPL made centralized economic power its enemy in Minnesota just as it did in North Dakota and they ran a candidate for governor in 1918 who made a name for himself attacking such power in Congress, whether it was against the autocratic Speaker of the House Joe Cannon or in his book criticizing the Federal Reserve.

But Charles A. Lindbergh Sr. lost to incumbent J.A.A. Burquist for the GOP nomination for governor in 1918 by a 199,325 to 150,626 vote tally. Even though Burquist had sent in National Guard forces to break up a violent miner's strike on the Range in 1916, Lindbergh couldn't get much labor support to offset his losses in farm country.[11] His name was smeared up and down the state by the Public Safety Commission, a body created by state government during the World War I to ostensibly to protect the "homeland," that turned into a force to crush dissent within the state, especially from Lindbergh.[12] It was tough enough already for Lindbergh, representing the rural 6th Congressional District that extended from Stearns County in central Minnesota straight north to the Canadian border, to try to appeal to urban voters with no urban background to speak of, but to also disprove rapid-fire charges of treason, disloyalty and so-called pro-German tendencies on his part was even worse. Many towns barred him from campaigning in them.[13] All he carried was the L, the Norwegian and German farmers mostly in the west and south (GOP efforts to purge disloyal Republicans around this time created bitter feelings in western Minnesota that sent voters into the arms of the NPL, Farm-Labor and eventually the Democrats where their loyalties lie for the most part to this day), while the laborers did not rally to his cause. [13]

Later that summer, Townley realized that what worked in a state that was 90 percent rural like North Dakota would not do so in Minnesota with its significant labor force. So he reached out to the unions in the Minnesota State Federation of Labor to form a loosely tied labor-based wing of the NPL. It was thus on Aug. 24, 1918, that the Farm-Labor Party was born at a meeting in St. Paul.[14]

Ultimately, one faction gobbled up the other and soon it was this new labor group that started to run the show. The League began to fall apart in the early 1920s as the recession robbed the organization of the dues money it needed to operate. Splits over policy and tactics also soon followed as the group grew. Perhaps the most contentious of these faction fights was over whether the NPL should continue to work within the framework of the two-party system or form its own independent political party. The traditional NPLers wanted the former and the new Laborites the latter. Given that energy and youth were on the side of the Laborites, they convinced the party leadership that the time for a new political party was at hand given the domination of the Republicans and the weakness of the Democrats. And the Laborites had election results on their side. In 1922 their endorsed candidates won three seats in Congress: Henrik Shipstead was elected to the United States Senate and Knud Wefald and O.J. Kvale were both elected to the House of Representatives that fall.

By 1924, it was inevitable that the old NPL group would be rolled into the new party with labor backing, but there were still bitter feelings and a clear urban-rural divide that threatened its cohesiveness. Both sides knew deep down that they had to work together in order to accomplish what they wanted. But the need was there for a bridge that could link town and country, farmer and union member, into an effective political party.

It was there and then that Floyd B. Olson reported for duty.

Renaissance Man

To be a "bridge" to different factions within a political party or group requires one important characteristic, that you have no burning enemies on either side. One doesn't have to be liked, just not hated with a passion.

No old NPL members or new members of the Farm-Labor coalition hated Floyd B. Olson. How could they? When the party was being built from 1918-1924, Olson was with the major parties. After graduating from Northwestern Law College in 1915, Olson went to work right away for a prestigious Minneapolis law firm of Larrabee and Davis. He sought the Democratic Party nomination for his local Congressional seat in 1918 and 1920. He was a supporter of President Wilson and the war effort, even joining the National Guard (although the Nye Committee's findings helped to change his mind on the war). Republican members of the Hennepin County Board thought highly enough of him as a lawyer to hire him as assistant district attorney in 1919 and they promoted him to the top job in 1920 when his boss, William Nash, was deposed for corruption.

But Olson, throughout his political career, always balanced his political pragmatism with a streak of radicalism and vise versa to advance himself. Thus, he spoke out against the conviction of law firm colleague James Peterson for sedition after he had spoke out against U.S. involvement in World War I. He attacked the Citizen's Alliance, a civic organization of businessmen in Minneapolis determined to keep closed shop unions out of their establishments, for using spies and agent provocateurs to infiltrate local unions. He was on the Group of

48, a committee formed to drum up interest in a potential Robert LaFollette Sr. presidential candidacy in 1919. He prosecuted members of the local branch of the Ku Klux Klan. He also won acclaim for convening a grand jury on a rapid increase of coal prices that accused the railroads of colluding to increase shipping rates and forced the Interstate Commerce Commission to intervene. That helped to win him labor support. He also impressed small merchants and other small businessmen, political reformers and progressive farmers with his prosecution of corrupt aldermen and city officials that ultimately cleaned-up Minneapolis. Persons also noted that as DA he targeted local big shots. Little shots, like a bank teller convicted of petty embezzlement, were given a slap on the wrist.[15]

So when the Farm-Labor Party met in St. Cloud for its 1924 nominating convention, Olson was its logical candidate for governor to balance both parts of the party's name. Olson used his connections in the Twin Cities to dominate those delegations and used an endorsement from Lindbergh (who died later that year of a brain tumor) to gain support from the rural delegations. However, charges of opportunism and enough obstinacy from old NPLers kept the convention from endorsing any candidate. He had to win the primary over Tom Davis, one of the first Farm-Labor candidates back in 1918, which he did by a slim 435-vote margin.[16]

Olson lost the general election to Theodore Christianson during the Republican sweep of that year. One thing that hurt Olson's candidacy was the charge of communist infiltration within some of the delegations at the state convention, so much so that even LaFollette would not run on the Farm-Labor line in the general elections or have anything to do with the party which split the leftist vote.[17] Still, Olson lost only by 43,000 votes and ran 26,000 votes ahead of LaFollette. He felt GOP scare tactics did him in, such as steel companies telling their workers on the Iron Range that they would lose their jobs if Olson was elected.[18] From that point onward, Olson made sure to present his pragmatist side to the voters. The F-L quickly dealt with the communist issue as soon as 1925 by passing a resolution banning any group advocating the violent overthrow of the U.S, government from being a part of the F-L coalition.[19] He also took time, during the years 1925-1930, to meet with fellow DAs across the state along with business, civic, and political leaders to assure them he was no wild-eyed radical which softened their opposition.[20] Olson heard the voters loud and clear: reform of the capitalist system yes, question it, no. However, this would not be the end of the issue.

By 1930 however, the issue of radicalism really didn't matter in the face of widespread economic ruin. The Great Depression gave the F-L the same chance in Minnesota it had given the NPL in North Dakota and the Progressives in Wisconsin, the chance to rule as desperate voters looked to anyone to help. By this time the F-L had gone from a mass movement, plenty of numbers but chaotic and formless, to a functioning, discipline party complete with dues and precinct organizations, caucus meetings to choose candidates, party officials and a biennial convention, structures that live on to this day in both major parties of the state.[21] Olson did a lot to help in this transformation and reaped its benefits. The old differences between rural and urban were finally submerged. The Scandinavians were firmly in his corner, especially as the Red River Valley became the F-L's power base. The Iron Range came on board and would soon stay that way. The labor unions of the Twin Cities were ready to do their part, and continue to do so to this day. Even the normally Republican-leaning Germans of the south would be there for a while, their farms and towns hurting in the Depression even though Olson supported World War I. Republican Ray Chase didn't have a chance in the face of this growing army. The first election where the F-L coalition was finally assembled saw Olson win 473,154 votes to Chase's 289,528. Now began the wild ride of the Farm-Labor Party's eight years in power.

The cooperative state

In some ways the F-L was like a traditional U.S. political party with a strong organization using patronage to feed its ranks. But in other ways, the set-up of the party rejected traditional U.S. models for mass European structures. Like the NPL, individual memberships could be had through a $3 due, but the F-L also allowed groups to affiliate themselves with it to provide the party muscle and financial support. These included labor unions of course, but also farmer's co-ops, professional groups like teachers, small merchants and business associations and student groups from universities across the state (the F-L used the University of Minnesota's research institutions to help formulate state policy on several different issues, just like the progressives used the University of Wisconsin, and created a solid bond between the party and the university community.[22]) Like European political parties, the F-L was class based and class conscious. It was the only independent political party of the Upper Midwest that was like that even among its Scandinavian supporters. Most of them were poorer farmers that lived in the Red River Valley or were the radical Finns of the Iron Range, their ranks bolstered with refugees from the losing side of the Finnish Civil War of 1918-1919 when Mannerheim and his Whites took power in that newly independent land.

While in office, Olson was no different than his counterparts in the Upper Midwest in what he signed into law: a two-year moratorium on farm foreclosures, relief measures for the Depression, old age pension laws, unemployment insurance. But he went beyond his counterparts in his help for labor unions. He signed into law a statute prohibiting court injunctions in labor disputes. He settled strikes personally like the Minneapolis trucker's strike, often in the worker's favor.[23] And he refused to send in the National Guard to settle a labor dispute in the Hormel meatpacker's strike in Austin in 1933 (something his distant future successor, Rudy Perpich, did do in another Hormel strike in the mid-1980s.)

Such measures helped Olson easily win re-election in 1932 and helped the F-L become the state's dominant party during the 1930s. They controlled both U.S. Senate seats, five U.S House seats and a majority of the legislature polled (in those days Minnesota state legislators were officially designated as non-partisan) along with the governor's mansion. But such absolute power, as often does, affected the minds of the F-L leadership, Olson included. And it sent them down paths of radicalism that have often been the bane of existence for the independent parties of the Upper Midwest.

But perhaps such radicalism was inevitable given the way the F-L was started and organized. As Minnesota unions began to affiliate with the radical Congress of Industrial Organizations (CIO), so too did leftist, radical union leaders begin to infiltrate the party. And being Scandinavian himself, Olson was well aware of the region's movement towards social-democracy, especially true after Sweden's socialists were elected to power in 1932. In the 1930s, the search was on for the elusive "third way," that route in between unbridled capitalism that seemed to have failed in the Depression and communist totalitarianism that was murdering millions in the Soviet Union and trying to wipe out Christianity. Could not the state and for that matter the region's cooperative businesses, those democracies of the boardroom, be a model for the rest of the country?

Riding high by the election of 1934, Olson completely forgot his pragmatism and went whole hog in other direction. The Farm-Labor platform, endorsed at the party's nominating convention in the spring of that year, has been considered by political scientists one of the most radical ever presented by a group holding major statewide party status.[24] In it, all mines, banks, utilities, transportation and factories were to be nationalized into public cooperatives and taxes were to be raised on the wealthy. Income was to be redistributed in classic socialist fashion. In his nomination acceptance speech, Olson left no doubt where he stood on this platform. He called for a "cooperative commonwealth wherein the party will stifle as much as possible the greed and avarice of the private profit system and bring a more equitable distribution of the wealth produced by the hands and minds of the people. I am frank to say I am what I want to be. I am a radical." [25]

Olson played to a convention whose delegates had become more radicalized as the Depression and drought wore on and who felt the prescriptions to resuscitate the capitalism system through the New Deal didn't seem to be bearing much fruit.[26] This convention and its platform, basically declared war on capitalism. This lead to the first splits within the party. The "right wing," or rural, former NPL types like Sen. Shipstead and Lt. Governor Hjalmar Peterson were opposed to the document while State Banking Commissioner Elmer G. Benson (who would later be appointed by Olson to the U.S. Senate in 1935) backing state's urban and Iron Range labor unions, supported it. This would be the split and the two men involved that would ultimately wreck the party by the late 1930s and 1940s. [27]

Olson ultimately won in 1934, helped by his successful intervention into a vicious Minneapolis truckers strike led by the Teamsters, through his popular efforts with foreclosure moratoriums for the state's farmers and through his own skills as a campaigner. The F-L's coalition of urban union votes from the Twin Cities counties of Hennepin and Ramsey along with the Iron Range vote in St. Louis County and the Norwegian vote in the Red River Valley held strong. But the margin of victory, 468,812 votes to Republican Martin Nelson's 396,359 and Democrat John Regan's 176,928 was a lot closer than his previous wins. Throughout the campaign, Olson had to alleviate the damage done to the F-L with such a radical programme, including going so far as having the party amend it during the campaign. He emphasized the socialist aspects of the platform, tried to cite figures as diverse as Franklin Roosevelt and Pope Pius XI for supporting his approach and highlighted differences between the F-L and the communists to assure voters that he wasn't going to confiscate small farms and businesses.[28]

But the damage was done. The issue of communism was introduced against the F-L in the 1934 campaign to which they never recovered. The textbook controversy was a case in point.[29] When the F-L, in one of its planks, called for the state itself to write and print the textbooks Minnesota school children would read, protests across the state erupted like Mt. St. Helens, especially from Lutheran, Baptist and Methodist ministers who feared radicals within the Olson Administration would begin to write such books with their own distorted views of history and propaganda in mind. Olson and his team were able to put the fire out on that issue for the 1934 campaign, but the social issue concerning Marxist infiltration into American society, whether through education or popular culture or the arts, was born and continues in various forms to this very day. It was also at this point that many farmers, particularly the Germans of southern Minnesota who voted for Olson in 1930 and '32, were pulled by their natural conservatism back to the GOP. Increases in prices and increases in horror at the F-L's platform of nationalization took them out of the Farm-Labor coalition.

The next big disaster to hit the F-L was the death of Olson himself. By 1936, the governor was more than exhausted trying to keep the fractious party, with its constant patronage and personal battles, together while also dealing with an increasingly balky legislature.[30] National politics, particularly the U.S. Senate seemed to beckon and with Olson a favorite of the Roosevelt Administration, it could grease his way to top of the national politic ladder. He decided to leave the governor's office behind for a Senate one. But he would never get his chance. Diagnosed with cancer in the spring of that year, Olson died on Aug. 22. Over 200,000 people showed up for his funeral in St. Paul where Wisconsin Governor Phil LaFollette gave the eulogy. F-L state Attorney General Harry Peterson said that 99% of the success of the Farm-Labor party was due to Olson, a fact born out as the party slowly collapsed without him.[31]

Benson, the F-L candidate for governor, benefited from a sympathy vote for Olson (and FDR's massive landslide of that year) that put him into office with 680,342 votes to Nelson's 431,841, but it would be the last statewide win for the party. Benson was Olson was out the common touch or any kind of pragmatism whatsoever.[32] A small-town banker from Appleton, Minn. who was radicalized by the Depression, Benson played to the ultra-leftists within his party and by the time he was elected, their influence was growing. Different factions of socialists and communists tried to worm their way into the F-L through their association with unions, student groups and co-op stores and businesses (Finnish co-ops especially where "Red Star"[33] products were sold in northeast Minnesota and northwest Wisconsin.) Their efforts were more complicated than one might expect given their own internal differences at that time.

"Socialists and communists were divided between the possiblists and the impossiblists," Hy Berman said. "The impossibilists wanted armed revolution and saw nothing to be gained by working with capitalist political parties. The possibilists though they could best advance their agenda and platform through working electorally with other parties. How the socialists and communists approached the political system depended upon which faction had the upper hand and at what time and what the international bodies that they were affiliated with were saying." [34]

By the time of 1936, the possibilists were definitely in charge. The 1935 "Popular Front" thesis of the Comintern gave the green light for ultra-leftists to work within the system and they did so with the Farm-Labor Party. There was nothing to stop them since the party platform only forbade those from membership who supported the violent overthrow of the U.S. government. With the Popular Front, the ultra-leftists could now step over that plank. But they were also allowed in through a welcoming environment by Benson, who gave such radicals jobs in his administration. Indeed, it may have been one of the few, if not only times in American history that communists were openly (stressing the world openly) close to the levers of power in any local, state or national government.[35] Benson felt he needed all the allies he could get against the myriad of enemies inside and outside the party. Such influence was also reflected the growth in power of the radical CIO among the state's unions.[36]

Many have said that the 1938 gubernatorial election was one of the dirtiest in Minnesota history. The Republicans, working in tandem with the Citizens Alliance, smelled victory, or blood if you want to call it that, in the air that year as an economic slump and Roosevelt's unpopular court-packing scheme turned the nation against the Democrats. Farm-Labor's social-democratic wing led by Peterson and Shipstead were alarmed by and attacked the leftist course the party was taking. Benson had to fend off Peterson in the primary and then answer all the attacks that came his way about his leftist ties and policies. He also had to deal with a persistent whisper campaign against "communist Jews" and other anti-Semitic language attacking Gov. Olson's advisors, his old Jewish friends from the neighborhood that Benson had kept on, and defended them in the face of such ugly and vicious attacks. [37]

But as red-baiting campaigns go, this one did not have to dig as deep to find such evidence. All one had to do was quote the Farm-Labor's platform from 1934 or Olson's statement on radicalism and their plans of nationalization to confirms such fears. Or they could see the communists in the Benson administration for confirmation or see F-L Eighth District Congressman John Bernard vote against American neutrality in the Spanish Civil War to back the Stalin-supported Spanish Republican government.[38] Or they could hear Benson's own words when he practically endorsed the takeover of a committee room inside the St. Paul capitol building by a radical group known as the "People's Lobby" in 1937 by saying "it's all right to be a little rough once in a while." [39]

There were two levels to the Republican campaign. One was

below-the-belt and the other was highbrow. The highbrow part was led by Dakota County DA Harold Stassen. He made a name for himself at 31 by beating out several old warhorses for the GOP nomination. He was also responsible for helping to establish a new "liberal" wing to the Republican Party in response to the dominance of FDR's Democrats. Stassen wasn't going to tear-up all of the programs that Olson and the F-L instituted, just run them better, more efficiently.[40] He also, unlike a lot of GOP stalwarts, was international in his outlook and rejected the Northern and Midwestern GOP's support for tariffs and isolationism. Indeed, he was re-elected in 1942 despite the fact he volunteered to join the Navy during World War II. Plus, his anti-communism became a selling point that Republicans would make good use of in the future and was a pole for non-communist leftists to align with. This form of Republicanism quickly became an attractive alternative because it allowed one to enjoy the pleasures of the New Deal without the logical consequences. It allowed Shipstead to abandon the F-L that year and join the GOP.[41] Party leaders, while not liking Stassen's views, were so determined to get the F-L out of office and so determined to succeed in this new political environment after nearly being voted to extinction for the past six years, dropped all their litmus tests. Stassen's overwhelming election and the overwhelming Republican state-wide sweep that followed, he won with 678,839 votes to Benson's 387,263, made himself a future presidential candidate (many times over) and was the precursor for the candidacies of Wendell Willkie, Thomas Dewey, Dwight Eisenhower and Richard Nixon. Stassen even worked to get Willkie the GOP nomination in 1940.[42]

Meanwhile the Farm-Labor Party saw its share of the vote total drop from 58 percent in 1936 to 34 percent two years later with an incumbent governor.[43] The question now was over the future and even while the 1938 campaign was going on, work quietly began on a project that would ultimately reduce the F-L to a museum piece in the U.S. political landscape, just as it did the Non-Partisan League and the Progressives.

The Urge to Merge

If you wonder, as some do, why the two major parties dominate 95 percent of the electorate, perhaps this article written on Aug.16, 2004 in the Washington Post by Pradeep Chhibber and Ken Kollman, both political science professors from the University of California-Berkley and the University of Michigan respectively, may have the answer:[44]

"Politicians and voters follow power. The decline in voting for minor parties after 1930 has corresponded to the increasing power of the national government relative to the states. The adoption of a national income tax and subsequent expansion of the federal government with the New Deal created pressures to develop fully national political parties. As the federal government gained more authority relative to the states and localities, voters wanted their votes to go for parties that would have a say in the great national questions of the day, rather than on the issues raised in state or local politics."

In other words, if you're looking for a culprit, blame Franklin D. Roosevelt.

Roosevelt's New Deal was the final layer of the birthday cake started during War Between the States to expand the power of the federal government and change the vision of the country from that of its founders, i.e., states and hundreds of localities and individuals living as independent communities and persons outside the limited established powers of the central government to provide a check on such powers, to one where the central government in Washington D.C. became the all-powerful matrix from hence all governments took their marching orders. The Articles of Confederation and the Constitution gave way to the Gettysburg Address.

The independent political parties of the Upper Midwest simply had no place within this framework. Whether intended or not or just measures trying to deal with the misery of the Depression by any means necessary, the "alphabet soup" agencies of the federal government became the sources of money for cash-strapped state and local governments and with that money came power itself. Also coming down from on high were nationalized laws on labor and housing and business to regulate a whole American economy, not 48 of them as had been done in the past. For the two main economic interest groups of the Upper Midwest, farmers and laborers, that meant attention had to be paid to Washington D.C. because it was in the nation's capital that laws were written that allowed unions to organize and be protected during strikes, or paid out farm subsidies, provided price floors for commodities and wrote trade deals with other countries.

When the states were truly the "laboratories of democracy," Governors like LaFollette, Langer, and Olson, could instill their own welfare states or reforms and new institutions and benefit themselves and their independent parties. Roosevelt and the New Deal snatched the state's power of innovation away from them, modeling the U.S. after what he did as Governor of New York. World War II only furthered that concentration and kept Roosevelt in power an extra eight years to solidify its control. And when it came to the "nation" as a whole, there were only two political parties of concern, Republicans and Democrats. These political parties could offer resources of money and political expertise to their state parties in case hard times set in for them (such as Illinois Republicans and Texas Democrats of today for example). The Farm-Labor Party and Progressives had no such national organizations to turn to when the hard times came in during the 1940s. And the national GOP was certainly not going to share its largess with the NPL.

The independent political parties of the Upper Midwest existed only because the Democrats were incredibly weak. In 1938, the Democratic Party's share of the Minnesota gubernatorial election vote was only 5.8 percent (in Wisconsin that election year the Democrat candidate for governor received 10 percent of the vote.). Even with the F-L weakened in 1940 and 1942, its gubernatorial nominee, Hjalmar Peterson, still tallied ahead of his Democrat counterpart, 459,609 votes to 140,021 in

1940 and a 299,917 to 75,151 in 1942. The Democrats in the Upper Midwest were weak because in the voters' mind they represented rebellion in the War Between the States (especially with the Southern states solid support for the Democrats afterward); because they were the party of Catholicism and the immigration of alien cultures into the WASP dominated U.S. and because they were controlled by big city political machines of the East like New York's Tammany Hall. Thus, the only support they had was in Catholic parts of Wisconsin, North Dakota and Minnesota. The Democrats were only useful a fusion party for groups like the Populists and or the NPL, or whatever faction of the Republican Party, stalwart of progressive, that was not in control.

The Depression, the New Deal and World War II changed all these voter perceptions. With Catholic and Protestant suffering alike during the 1930s from the poor economy and the drought in addition to the popularity of Fr. Coughlin, religious differences weren't quite so sharp anymore and became even less so when Catholic and Protestant were serving in the same foxholes in North Africa, Wake Island and Normandy beach. The same was true for Northerners and Southerners 80 years after the firing on Ft. Sumter. And the popularity of Franklin Roosevelt, even though he was nominated and renominated by nefarious and corrupt political bosses, recast the image of the Democratic Party. The Democrats were the party of farm price supports, Social Security, the Wagner Act, the repeal of Prohibition, the WPA and the CCC, the TVA, V-E and V-J days as well. While the NPL, Progressives and Farm-Labor were winning on the state level during the 1930s, Roosevelt and Harry Truman were carrying their states in presidential elections over a 12-year period. Ultimately this success and these new perceptions would filter downward.

Especially among the young. The generation that had lived through and survived the Depression and World War II were enamored of the Democratic Party given all that history. The pressure to force a merger between the NPL and the Democrats in North Dakota came from young men like Lloyd Omdahl and Quentin Burdick,[45] who became the new party's first elected Congressman and Senator in 1958 and 1960, In Wisconsin, young Gaylord Nelson, William Proxmire and Jim Doyle Sr., the father of current Wisconsin governor Jim Doyle Jr., steered former Progressive and Socialist Party members into Democratic column.[46] The same was oh so true in Minnesota. Students and professors at the state's private and public colleges had unique roles in the party as activists, advisors, campaign managers and workers in the Farm-Labor coalition, something that was carried on after the F-L merged with the Democrats all the way to Professor Paul Wellstone and his grassroots network that included many students.

"Student activism was very important to the organization of the DFL," Polk County, Wisconsin. Historian Margie Hallquist said. "Much of the university community was involved in politics when I attended school at Macalester in St. Paul. I was an activist for Congressmen Don Fraser and Eugene McCarthy and Hubert Humphrey too. I took his American History class for the 1943-44 school year at Macalester." [47]

Humphrey and his friend Orville Freeman were young students at the University of Minnesota caught up in the activism of the Farm-Labor Party.[48] They would be instrumental into merging that party with the Democrats by 1943.

The old folk would be left behind of course, obsolete and irrelevant. Langer and Robert LaFollette Jr. stuck by tradition and the old labels which meant sticking by the GOP. [49] Peterson tried to keep the F-L alive as best he could. But election defeat after election defeat, the destructive intra-party warfare between the radical and social democrat wings of the party and the determination of the Roosevelt Administration to bring the two parties together doomed his efforts. Peterson of course would point out that a leftist vote for the Democrats was vote for a party that in the South stood for white supremacy and

Negrophobia, especially amongst its populist elements. It was vote for a party that stood for Catholic censorship by the Legion of Decency, Catholic conservatism in social policy and Catholic authoritarianism in government. And it was a vote for a party still run by crooked political bosses, many of whom were supported by gangsters.[50] It would not be a happy vote.

All of this was true but it was balanced out by the fact that there was no home for any Progressive, NPL or F-L activist in the GOP either, especially after Robert LaFollette Jr. was unceremoniously dumped by his own party in a 1946 Senate primary defeat by one Joseph McCarthy.[51] The GOP was, is and ever shall be a business party. Those who spent decades condemning, taxing and trying to regulate business from the NPL, Farm-Labor or Progressive parties were not going to find it easy to be with the Republicans.

Even though the Democrats took a beating in the 1938 midterm elections, it wasn't all bad news for Roosevelt. The defeat of the Farm-Labor party and the Progressives in that same year contained the Dems' silver lining. After the election Roosevelt stated: "We have eliminated Phil LaFollette and the Farm-Labor people in the northwest as a standing third party threat. They must and will come to us if we remain definitely the liberal party."

Roosevelt had been interested in Minnesota since 1931. He knew Olson as a fellow governor, they thought alike in many ways and was impressed by Olson's accomplishments.[52] FDR also had to deal with a torn apart Democratic Party in the state between its Catholic wing, who were supporters of Roosevelt's rival Al Smith, and progressive wing that supported Roosevelt and got a lion's share of the patronage when FDR was elected.[53] Indeed, this split had first come out into the open at the 1932 Democratic Convention in Chicago where a credentials challenge over the Minnesota delegation was test of strength between Smith and Roosevelt.[54] The split persisted well into the 1930s and kept the party from expanding upon FDR's victories there.

"The merger of the Democrats and the Farm-Labor party was

forced by the Roosevelt Administration," Hy Berman said. "Many in both parties were unwilling to do it, but Roosevelt wanted Minnesota's electoral votes and wanted congressional support from the state. Those in the F-L that supported the merger wanted to back Roosevelt and the war as part of the Popular Front strategy."[55]

Much had to be ironed out between the two parties before a merger could successfully take place. The legal aspects of it were already starting to be studied in the aftermath of Benson's 1938 defeat.[56] Ultimately walls that would have prevented the merger from taking place broke down. After Pearl Harbor, with the U.S. coming into the war on the side of Soviet Union, the far left dropped its objections, hewing to the Popular Front line.[57] More defeats at the ballot box brought all the activists on board. A coalition of Catholic Democrats attracted to the social gospel, members of AFL and the Peterson wing of the F-L helped to elect John McDonough mayor of St.Paul in 1940. This election showed that a new coalition could work and provided even more momentum for the merger.[58] McDonough became a supporter of the merger as did another candidate, soon-to-be elected mayor of Minneapolis via the same broad coalition, Hubert Humphrey. By 1943, he and then vice-president Henry Wallace helped to bring all the factions finally together for the new Democratic-Farm Labor party.[59]

Reflections in the mirror

At this point, we could end the chapter here with the merger having done away with the Farm-Labor Party for good (though some leftists have tried to revive the label outside Minnesota to no avail.) But since this is a book that also looks at cultural impacts upon politics, it is a good idea to reflect upon how the Minnesota DFL became a mirror to the Democrats nationally, a mirror to the liberal consensus that existed up until it was finally shattered in 1980 and how the party itself carried on until its death in 2002.

From the time of the merger until the time Orville Freeman

was first elected governor in 1954, the DFL worked long and hard to produce the grassroots machine and coalitions that allowed it to become the dominant party in the state until 1990. During this 36-year period, the GOP controlled the governor's office for only 10 years and only because voters felt it was a brake whenever the DFL became too arrogant in power. Thus in 1978, 40 years after Harold Stassen came to office in a Republican sweep, the Republicans duplicated the feat (known in Minnesota as the "Election Night Massacre") with largely the same Stassen model. However, four years later, the GOP was swept out of office again in a DFL landslide as if the natural order of things was restored.

The first thing Hubert Humphrey and company had to do was to take away the taint of communism and radicalism the new party inherited from the F-L. That required five years of struggle to purge the party of such influences, in sometimes heated fashion, until 1948 when the Wallace third-party run for President gathered such elements into its fold and allowed Truman to carry Minnesota and Humphrey to be elected to the Senate. [60] When this was done, the Dems could rebuild the F-L coalition of small farmers, particularly in the Red River Valley, small merchants, managers, union laborers, students and university and college administrators. (As it became the state's dominant party, it began to attract big business support as well.) This coalition represented the liberal consensus: a tough, anti-communist foreign policy without being warlike, supporting civil rights, protecting and expanding the welfare state at home, supporting internationalism abroad and, as it may seem surprising today, a fairly conservative social policy.[61] It was the local DFL leadership that got the alcoholic and ner'-do-well husband of Cora Knudtsen, the state's first female representative in the U.S Congress, to write a letter published statewide and picked up nationally asking "Cora, come home." that cost Knudtsen her seat during the 1958 election.

An old LTV Steel dump truck from its closed mine in Hoyt Lakes, Minn. now rests at Mineview in the Sky outside of Virginia, Minnesota on the Iron Range

It also represented the Democratic Party in the North and West and allowed this small state to have weight and influence in party affairs way beyond it population base, far more so than bigger states like New York, Texas or California. When Humphrey made his famous, or infamous depending on your point of view, speech at the Democratic National Convention of 1948, calling for the Democratic Party "to get out of the darkness of state's right and into the light of human rights," he became a figure of hatred in Southern Democratic circles for years because his rise to prominence signaled the South's fall from power in the Democratic Party, a party they founded and nurtured and kept alive for years. The 1948 campaign was the first in which Southerners looked for alternatives to the Democratic Party, whether in third party candidates like Strom Thurmond in 1948, Harry F. Byrd in 1960 and George Wallace in 1968 or ultimately follow Thurmond into the Republican Party. Just as World War II broke down stereotypes and perceptions about the Democratic

Party in the North, it did the same to Southerners in regards to the Republican Party in the South and it became a viable alternative.

By representing a perfect reflection of the liberal consensus, the DFL was able to place its best politicians and leaders in high office nationally. Both Humphrey and his protégé Walter Mondale served as vice-president and both mounted campaigns for the top job as well. A DFLer was on a Democratic presidential ticket in five out of six elections from 1964 through 1984. Freeman had one of the longest terms as Secretary of Agriculture, eight years, serving the Kennedy and Johnson Administrations. Another DFLer, Congressman Bob Berglund from the Seventh District, served as Ag Secretary in the Carter Administration. Governor Wendell Anderson made the cover of Time in 1973 for the story "Living the Good Life in Minnesota." But that consensus would start to break apart in the 1960s and 70s and the man who put a sledgehammer to it was another DFL icon, Eugene McCarthy.

McCarthy was an iconoclastic, witty, thoughtful, civilized but also aloof, diffident and vain congressman and senator first elected in 1948 out of St. Paul. He was a part of the ticket balancing process that the major parties always engaged in.

"Mondale and Berglund were there to appeal to Scandinavians, Freeman to Anglos, McCarthy to Catholics and (Congressman John) Blatnik to Slavs," Hy Berman said. "It was group of men picked to best represent the state and national society." [62]

But McCarthy, a man of deep and residing faith instilled into him by the German Benedictine monks of St. John's College just outside of St. Cloud in heavily German Catholic Stearns County, resented being the "house Catholic" of the DFL along with that kind of traditional ethnic politics.[63] He began to reflect the views of his Fifth District that included many young professionals and students who began to critique the liberal consensus and didn't like what they saw. McCarthy's split with Humphrey, which began with the Vietnam War and McCarthy's candidacy for president in 1968, began the splits that ultimately tore apart the DFL coalition in the state and the Democratic Party nationally. Fights over foreign policy, abortion, gay rights and development within the Arrowhead's vast wilderness preserves mirrored those in the national party as well. As this was going on, changing demographics and economics in the 1980s and 90s was transforming the state and putting an end to the traditional DFL coalition.

Just like the rest of the nation, Minnesota's economy mirrored the transition between an ag/industrial model to that supporting the service industries and it meant a decline in the DFL's base in those areas. The loss of small farmers in the 1980s and 90s coincided with the collapse of the party in many rural areas of the state. More of their voting base was lost when union labor employment left the state or disappeared altogether when mines were shut down on the Iron Range or when the meatpacking union at the Hormel plant in Austin was wrecked after a strike in the mid-1980s. At the same time, the service economy began to take office in the outer-ring suburban and exurban areas of the Twin Cities. The state has gone through a building boom in these areas from the 1980s onward to service this economy with office-park dads and soccer moms replacing Norwegian bachelor farmers and Slavic mine workers and their families. Companies like Honeywell and Minneapolis-Moline are gone now and Pillsbury and General Mills are now owned by the same conglomerate. 3M (Minnesota Mining and Manufacturing) is still around, but the company that is most celebrated in the state today is Medtronics, a medical supplies company well positioned to take advantage of the expanding health care field as the Baby Boomers retire. Living in the newly developed subdivisions from Maple Grove to Blaine to Woodbury to Chanhassen, are newcomers looking for that ever elusive good life; city dwellers looking for space and escape from rising crimes rates that plagued both Minneapolis and St. Paul in the late 1980s and early 90s and refugees from the Iron

Range, rural Minnesota and rural parts of western Wisconsin, Iowa and the Dakotas looking for work. Other newcomers also include immigrants, both legal and illegal, working cheap and sometimes invisible on the state's farms and factories of southern Minnesota and in jobs supposedly nobody wants (or wants to pay for better still) in the Twin Cities area or the Hmong, our former indigenous allies during the Vietnam War, resettled into the United States.

All of these changes saw the DFL's voter base shrink while the GOP's grew over time. And this was not your father or your grandfather's GOP (the state's Republicans were so embarrassed by their party's label that they started calling themselves Independent Republicans right after the Watergate scandal) or Harold Stassen's for that matter. When Vin Weber was elected in 1978 to the U.S. House of Representatives in the Second District in southern Minnesota, it was a signal that the postwar intellectual and political conservative movement had arrived in the state and it began to push liberal and moderate members right out of the party. Weber became one of the most prominent conservatives elected in Minnesota in years and was part of a band of young House Republicans elected in the late 1970s and early 80s that ultimately set the ideological tone for the GOP in Congress by the time the party took power in 1995. This ideology also trickled down to the state level. The GOP took control of the state's House of Representatives in 1984 due in large part to get-out-the-vote work done by anti-abortion groups like Minnesota Concern Citizens for Life which gave the GOP for the first time a network of grassroots political organizations that could mobilize voters more effectively than the old party structures could. The rise of talk radio on the AM dial in the Twin Cities gave conservatives a media outlet unlike any before that they could both get their message across unfiltered and promote political leaders. But the most important factor in the rise of conservatism in the state was that the DFL and the state socialism they represented became victims of their own success.

"What's hurt the DFL more than anything has been the rise of incomes in the state," Dane Smith said. "It used to be Minnesota was in the high 20s nationally when it came to income and by the turn of the century, the state shot up into the top 10. That happened under a tax code that leans heavily on income taxes rather than property or sales taxes, given the old Farm-Labor party's bias against rich people. Well, a lot of middle class people were seeing their incomes rise during the 1980s and 90s boom, buying expensive houses in the suburbs and big ticket items and started moving up into higher tax brackets. And paying more in taxes has a way of making someone a conservative pretty quick." [64]

By 2003, the conservative triumph within the GOP was complete. They controlled the party and the party controlled state government. Prominent moderates and liberals who were state office holders like Judy Dutcher or Dean Johnson switched parties or, like former governor Arne Carlson, became independents. Rudy Boschwitz, best expressed this shift in the political wind direction. Considered a moderate when first elected (he supported Howard Baker for President in 1980 instead of Ronald Reagan), he became quite conservative when he ran against Wellstone for the second time in 1996. The real differences in the state's GOP have more to do with location (rural vs. suburban) and style or points of emphasis than any differences in philosophy.

At the other end of the spectrum, Paul Wellstone became an important symbol of the DFL during the 1990s, but he had amazingly little impact on state party campaigns or its ideology during this time. Part of the reason was that, being a U.S. Senator, Wellstone had precious little time despite his enormous energy to devote to state party matters (what Lyndon Johnson used to call "chickenshit politics.") Another reason was that those in the DFL who tried to run Wellstone-like campaigns were beaten badly, lacking in Wellstone's political talents and grassroots network connections. That meant business as usual within the DFL establishment which meant running on names, like that Humphrey, Freeman and Mondale - the sons of all three of the founding fathers of the DFL all ran for governor in 1998 – or running veteran politicians like long-time State Senate Majority Leader Roger Moe. Because of this, the DFL was still seen as the establishment party of Minnesota and that left them vulnerable to third party populists looking to take their beefs out on them.

Because the state's campaign finance laws allow for public funding for parties that get five percent of the state's vote, the Green and Reform/Independence parties chopped into what was left of the DFL's shrinking voter base. Ralph Nader's runs for president helped to build up the Green party locally and it began to score successes electing candidates to township boards, county councils and city councils in Minneapolis and Duluth ("the Greens practically run the Duluth City Council," Dane Smith said.) [65] They took votes from the DFL's left. The Reform/Independence Party was started by Dean Barkley, a small businessman who has been a pain-in-the-ass to the DFL establishment ever since he was a George McGovern supporter in 1972 campaigning against native son Hubert Humphrey because of the Vietnam War. Barkley had gotten disgusted with the big money floating in the DFL circles. Having been out of politics for some time, Barkley got back in inspired by Ross Perot. He ran for the U.S. House in 1992 and the Senate in 1994 and 1996. He helped to found the Minnesota chapter of the Reform Party and made it one of the most organized out of all the state Reform parties in the nation. This paid off in 1998 when Jesse "The Body" Ventura "shocked the world" and became Minnesota's governor, taking fiscally conservative but socially liberal voters in the Twin Cities suburbs away from the DFL. A former DFL Congressman, Tim Penny, was the party's (their name was changed to Independence after the intra-party brawls during the 2000 presidential election) nominee for governor in 2002.

There are still those to this day who want to believe that if Rick Kahn, Wellstone's campaign treasurer and longtime friend, had been somewhere else instead of at the Paul Wellstone Memorial inside Williams Arena on the campus of the University of Minnesota on Oct. 28, 2002 - maybe doing missionary work in Borneo perhaps, or being a part of a polar expedition in the Artic or maybe just at a Minnesota Timberwolves game - that somehow, the DFL would have swept to victory a few days later. They want to believe that if he had just kept his emotions in check or just plain kept his mouth shut, then Mondale would be in the Senate, Moe would be governor and Wellstone's legacy would be upheld. They want to believe all this because Rick Kahn did not keep his mouth shut and turned his funeral eulogy into a campaign speech exhorting Wellstone's followers to the polls to vote for the DFL and calling on the GOP to concede the race. This embarrassed the Republicans who attended and caused Ventura to walk out. Had he just zipped it tight, then all would be right in the world and the Democrats would have won in November across the board and even across the country.

Such sentiments are ones expressed by people in denial. Any astute political observer could have looked at the DFL's election results since 1988 and looked at the demographic trends and put two and two together realized that the DFL's day of reckoning was coming. Any young volunteer working for the Wellstone campaign could have told DFL leaders that putting Walter Mondale in his place on the ticket to go with Moe, State Senate Majority leader and a 30-year member of that body, and Hubert H. "Buck" Humphrey IV, the senator's grandson running for secretary of state, would make their jobs a lot harder trying to motivate voters, many of whom were barely alive during Mondale's prime. And any Republican could of said privately they didn't need any more motivation from Rick Kahn to vote for the GOP which they were already planning to turn out to do anyway.

It's not that Mondale did a bad job in the 2002 campaign. In fact, given the circumstances, he accounted for himself quite well. It's the message that DFL leaders sent by picking Mondale over, say, state auditor and recent convert from the GOP Judy Dutcher or state supreme court justice and Vikings' hall of famer Alan Page, that reinforced the feeling in the minds of many of the state's voters that the DFL was grandma and grandpa's political party. Coleman, one of the few if any neoconservatives elected to public office, now had a message for his campaign other than being anti-Wellstone: "I'm the present and the future and the DFL is the past."

There is no future for the DFL. The Democratic Party will continue to have a future in Minnesota (in fact they did quite well in the 2004 election, winning the state for John Kerry and making big gains in the state House of Representatives thanks to a lack of Green and Independence Party candidates on the ballot) but the DFL will not. Tuesday, November 5, 2002 was the day it officially died. The party that traced its roots back to Charles Lindbergh Sr., Arthur C. Townley, and Floyd B. Olson, brought to prominence by Hubert Humphrey, Orville Freeman, Walter Mondale, Eugene McCarthy, Wendell Anderson and Paul Wellstone ceased that night because the electoral coalition that it always relied on, small farmers, white ethnics, union miners on the Iron Range and union industrial workers in the Twin Cities, cannot win statewide elections anymore. This author wrote the party's epitaph in the January 2003 issue of *Chronicles*:

"Unfortunately suburbanization, globalization, the decline of family farms and manufacturing jobs and the left's lurch towards cultural Marxism affected Minnesota just as they did the rest of the country. The election results declare that Minnesota has officially become suburbia just like everywhere else - and the Democrats will adjust accordingly. There are far more soccer moms and office-park dads in the Land of 10,000 Lakes than there are farmers, factory workers and the Scandinavian socialists who once formed the DFL's backbone."

The Democrats will hunt for votes where the ducks are, in the suburbs and exurbs of the Twin Cities and within the "arc," the line extending from Duluth to St. Cloud to Rochester where three-quarters of the state's voters live, leaving out much of their former voting base. State Attorney General Mike Hatch will try to sell a "suburban populist" message to voters in not only in traditional 'burbs like, Woodbury and New Brighton, but new 'burbs like New Prague and Cambridge. They will also look for votes in the exploding Third-World immigrant populations within the state. State Senator Mee Moua, the first female Hmong member of that body, has more of a claim on the party's future than "Buck" Humphrey or any other offspring of the party's founders. And with the decline and fall of the DFL establishment, the ire of Dean Barkley and his Independence Party has now gone away and they will quietly return to the DFL fold (moderates need not apply to the state GOP) completing its transformation.

Dane Smith says there's a quiet movement within the party to drop the F-L from the nameplate, but the labor activists still quite dominant in party affairs won't hear of it. Of course there's a catch: the dominant labor activists are not the Teamsters, UAW, Farmer's Union or United Steelworkers of America (on the Iron Range) of yore. They are AFSCME and the NEA, teachers and government employees, what's left of labor after globalization.

As a famous Minnesotan once sung: "The times they are a changing."

Chapter 5—The Progressives

"Whatever may be the limitations which trammel inquiry elsewhere, we believe that the great state University of Wisconsin should ever encourage that continual and fearless sifting and winnowing by which alone the truth can be found."[4]

One could start the study of the Progressive Party in Wisconsin and the progressive movement in general in the state's capital city of Madison. It seems like the right place. The city's main thoroughfare, State Street, connects the University of Wisconsin and the state capital building itself. It was down this seven block path that UW political science and sociology professors walked to the capital at the invitation of governor-elect Robert M. LaFollette in 1901 to help him develop policies for political and economic reform that still remain to this day in the Badger State.[5] And the fact that LaFollette would seek out advice from academia rather than businessmen or political hacks to develop public policy, in other words government by "experts," defined the progressive movement itself. Policies would be drawn up by those learned in the areas of finance, sociology or engineering instead of those who had a personal or business stake in them. LaFollette's election in 1900, which grabbed power from the state's business community (i.e.

railroads) for the first time since the War Between the States, was truly momentous not just for the state itself but for the progressive movement nationally. Locally it was known and still is known today as the "Wisconsin Idea," defined by the phrase "fearless sifting and winnowing" of ideas the university prides itself on.[3]

LaFollette seemed to epitomize the Progressive lifestyle and that of Madison itself. He was born and raised in Dane County, practiced law there and lived in a comfortable middle class home in the Madison suburb of Maple Bluff.[4] He was a graduate of the UW and went to school there during a time of great reform of its methods and operation along with a revamping of its curricula by its then president and one of LaFollette's mentors Charles Van Hise. LaFollette was also a prominent speaker on the Chautauqua circuit that was a part of progressive culture of that time.

Madison may well have been the Rome of the progressive movement in Wisconsin. But like Rome, it would have been nothing without an Athens or a greater Greek culture to build its civilization upon. Likewise, the progressive movement and the party it eventually founded in the 1930s would have been confined to middle and upper middle class Madison had it not been for a place in northwest Wisconsin - a region known as the Indianhead by the shape of its geography - that helped to provide the political energy, activism, and ultimately power for those Madison progressives to enact their ideas. In the center of the Indianhead, a seeming wilderness of lakes, rivers, farms, swamps and woods, is Polk County. And just like Orange County, California powered the postwar conservative movement, just like Cook County, Illinois powered the Democratic Party of that state and Nassau County, New York served the same purpose to Empire State Republicans, so to did Polk serve the progressives of Wisconsin.

At Ground Zero

1933 in Wisconsin was the year of the milk strikes. Dairy farmers, angry at the low prices they were receiving for their milk, decided to do something about it. Starting on Feb. 15, farmers refused to sell their milk to local dairies or have it shipped to other parts of the country. In fact, they dumped it, vast gallons of it, all over the ground. Given that Wisconsin was the leading producer of surplus milk and dairy products in the country, the situation was serious.

This was particularly true in the eastern part of the state and just like the draft riots that occurred during the War Between the States, once again the mostly German-Catholic farmers in the east were aflame with revolt.[5] Clashes between strikers trying to prevent dairies from taking in milk not dumped in the strike and police, bombings, blockades and National Guard deployments showed a state in upheaval.

Most of the violent incidents took place in the eastern and southern parts of Wisconsin, a strange phenomenon since this was then considered (and still is) the most conservative part of the state. But then again desperate times produce desperate measures and Depression era farmers in Wisconsin and practically everywhere else were desperate. That was true in Polk County too, where dairy farmers were striking as well (although with less acrimony and turmoil.)

Given this environment, not everyone was going to sympathize with the farmers' cause. The local small town newspapers in Polk County attacked the strikers in editorials and in news stories, tying them in with the violence occurring in the other parts of state, attacking their politics as "radical" and spreading rumors about incidents of vandalism and theft on the part of the strikers. Feeling unfairly mischaracterized, distorted and attacked in the local papers, farmers thought it was high time someone or something speak for them and their interests.

"A political subdivision that is more than 80 percent liberal and progressive deserves a mouthpiece that will be favorable to its aims and wishes." (One could imagine a conservative speaking the same way about talk radio.) [6]

Thus on Nov. 2, the *Inter-County Leader* was born, the first ever cooperative newspaper in the nation.

Cooperative businesses were organized all over the county in 1933. The movement started among the county's creameries in the 1900 and spread to other businesses by the time of the Great Depression. Polk's majority Scandinavian-based population was certainly not unfamiliar with the idea of co-ops and given their spread into businesses like dairy, dry goods, oil, retail and farm services, one could certainly say they were embraced.

"Oh there were a lot of co-ops in Polk County back then," county historian Marge Hallquist, whose father Harry was on the board of directors for the *Leader*, said. "D.D. Kennedy, who was a local farmer and state legislator, was involved in the co-op movement in Alberta in 1914 and was very active here in helping to organize them." [7]

This farmstead in Polk County located off of State Highway 48 has lasted from LaFollette's day to the present

Kennedy, along with Hallquist, was part of a network of organizers and activists active with both co-ops and the Farmer's Union. Membership in the Union was also strong in Polk County. Five of the seven members of the original board of the newspaper were members of the Union. While not affiliated with the Farmer's Union, the paper was certainly supportive of its aims. And that provided a readership base for the paper when it was officially launched. Subscribers not only provided a couple of bucks to get the newspaper every week, but to also buy memberships in the company that ran the paper and have voting power in making decisions in areas like hiring, advertising rates and, most important in regards to the *Leader's* founding, editorial content.

And much of that content in that first issue concerned the milk strike.

"No shortage of pickets in Polk County. In fact there were 50. [They were so numerous] that it became necessary to allow only five at a time to come from each town as otherwise there were too many." [8]

Given its expressed support for the strikers, one would think the newspaper would have a hard time finding local advertisers to fill its pages and pay its bills. But the local network of co-op businesses such as the People's Co-op Oil Association in Luck or the People's Garage in Milltown, provided the revenue the paper needed to keep going.

The first issue of the Leader contained stories on the milk strikes, the milk holiday movement and stories on strike meetings held in local villages. There was also a story written to dispel rumors and gossip on the strike and it also contained a feature story on a Norwegian farmer in Sun Prairie shot during the strikes written by Bill Evjue, editor of the progressive *Capital Times* newspaper of Madison. The paper wasn't shy about including stories from outside the boundaries of Polk County. The second edition of the paper had an article on a call for a national farmer's holiday (withholding of farm goods) at the national convention of the Farmer's Union in St. Paul. The actions of governors like Bill

Langer of North Dakota and Floyd B. Olson of neighboring Minnesota, such as placing moratoriums on farm foreclosures and sending relief aid to farmers not only suffering from low prices but the effects of drought as well, made the news. A speech by Sen. Robert LaFollette Jr. urging farmers to organize and attended by 1,500 persons in the eastern Wisconsin town of Hilbert, was reported on. Special columns were also published, like that on page 11 of issue one entitled "Who's Got Your Gold, The Government or a Group of Private Bankers?" written by Andre Nordskog criticizing the new Roosevelt administration's action confiscating all privately held stocks of gold in excess of $100 in exchange for private notes. Indeed, despite its promises and short duration, the new administration quickly came in for criticism by the paper as this editorial point out:

"After months of patient waiting, during which time the farmer and laborers of America have pressed to the Roosevelt administration petitions and resolutions setting for the immediate necessity for a rise in farm prices, we have now reached a point where we are fast losing confidence in the administration. This confidence has not been lost by any single act but by a series of acts which, in our judgment, indicate that the 'monied interests' of this country still dominate the government."

Such writing would suggest a radical newspaper which the early edition of the *Leader* was at that time. But this was not going to be a northwoods version of the *Daily Worker*. On the inside pages of the first edition of the *Leader* was a pastor's column written by Rev. Otto E. Klett, a local Lutheran cleric. It also, like any good small-town paper, wrote on the community news in places around the county like Dresser Junction:

"A number of young friends of Miss Evelyn Hayman were entertained at a Halloween party at her home Tuesday evening." It also told of upcoming community events: "A very fine program sponsored by the young folks at English Lutheran Church takes place Sunday evening." [9]

Beyond what talked about when it came to the milk strike and farmer's holidays and columns about the "monied interest" running Washington, the *Leader* was still a community newspaper with local stories, local advertisers and local readers. Evjue was impressed enough about the *Leader* to inform his readers in Madison of what was going on in Polk County.

"A new paper, a weekly, has started in Centuria to serve Polk and neighboring counties. The paper was started by farmers and others interested in having a paper that would represent the farmers' work strike. In the *Inter-County Leader*, the farmers of Polk and surrounding counties will have a publication that will give them a square deal." [10]

The strike came to an end on Nov. 23 but its ramifications lasted well into the next year, which was an election year.

Governor Albert Schmedeman was a Democrat elected in the Roosevelt landslide two years earlier and elected also because of a split in the dominant Republican Party. The state GOP dumped incumbent Phillip LaFollette in favor of Walter Kohler Sr. For LaFollette, to see his father's own party and the party of his brother, a sitting United States Senator, reject him like this was an insult and many Republicans of LaFollette's "progressive" wing voted for the Democrat Schmedeman rather than for Kohler, head of the "stalwart" faction, in revenge. But that wasn't the end of the story. LaFollette wanted to be governor again, but also did not want to engage in another destructive intra-party battle with the stalwarts. He also saw the GOP label as hardly an attractive one considering that the party was still blamed for the Depression, a tag that lasted in the popular mind for another 50 years. Perhaps a new party, made up of his own progressive faction from the GOP, progressives within the Democratic Party and the powerful Socialist political machine in Milwaukee, would be strong enough to carry the state.

Thus the top story in the May 3 edition of the *Leader* concerned a recent state Supreme Court decision. "Third-Party

Movement Valid," read the headline. The subheads said that the new Progressive Party could now start organizing for the next election. In Polk County, it didn't take long for this decision to spark a wildfire as the next week's edition of the *Leader* was dominated by news of the new party's first organizational meeting:

"The date for the Wisconsin third-party parley has been set for May 19 in Fond du Lac, where delegates from 71 counties of the state will meet and very likely launch the third party movement.

If the third party is actually gotten underway, there will be no love lost anywhere. The GOP will be glad to get rid of the Progressives and certainly we are unable to imagine any Progressive going around weeping over the divorcement from the party of Hoover, Mellon and Husband.

Polk County has already elected its delegate to the parley, Assemblyman Marius Dueholm..." [11]

Just as the Force runs strong through the Skywalker family of *Star Wars* fame, so to, does progressive politics run through the Dueholm family. Three generations of Dueholms, Marius, Harvey and Robert, served in the state Assembly from Polk County throughout the 20th century.

"Let's just say my family talked politics a lot." Robert, who served in the Assembly from 1995-1999, said. [12]

Not just talked but lived as well. How could he not attending LaFollette Elementary School, built in 1918 and named after not a deceased but still living U.S. Senator. Both Robert's father Harvey and all of Robert's siblings attended the school until it was closed in 1963. Marius had a hand in creating the school and both he and Harvey served on its board.

The school was located on County Highway O, just north of State Highway 48. Dueholm did not live too far away, just off of 48 on County Highway I in the Bone Lake region of Polk County. The area was settled by Danes, including Marius, who came to the United States when he was 11 in 1899.[13] At the same time that Haugenism swept Norway and the Baptist movement was strong in Sweden, so to, did Denmark go through its movement of social, religious and political change. The Grundvig Movement swept through the Lutheran churches of Denmark begun by a minister, one Nicolae Grundvig, in the 1850s. Like its counterparts throughout the rest of Scandinavia, the Grundvig movement focused itself on reforms and liberalization in church catechism, politics and social mores. Grundvigs emphasized all-around education through the folk school movement. Besides just book learning, folk school students would also exercise and learn to sing as well. The Polk County township of West Denmark had a Grundvig seminary and Bone Lake Lutheran Church was a Grundvig church.

The former Robert M. LaFollette Sr., Elementary School is located on County Highway O in Polk County

"You had a very educated population in this area among the immigrants and one influenced by the Scandinavian liberal church movements," JoAnne Hallquist, who, like her sister Marge, is a Polk County historian and who had a relative back in Denmark active in social democratic politics. "There were

Swedish Baptists in Trade Lake and Norwegian Free Churches in Amery and Garfield Township." [14]

Thus, the young arrivals to Polk County like Dueholm were both educated and influenced by the new ideas of the liberal church movements, a perfect base for this new Progressive Party to form around. Indeed, the chairman of the party in Polk County, a Dr. Anton Nelson, whose father emigrated from Sweden, had a relative of his in the Riksdag, the Swedish parliament.

"My grandfather and father both had a strong sense of neighborhood and neighbors," Dueholm said. "They believed that government should help people that need it and they believed that they had they had the obligation to leave the earth better than when they came into it." [15]

But politics itself is more than just a jigsaw puzzle fitting the right pieces into place. The Duehoims would have never been a success just fitting their ideology, religion and ethnicity onto the Polk County electorate. A personal touch was required as well.

"My father and grandfather sold wool goods in the county throughout the winter to subsidize their farming," Dueholm said. "Going from town to town across the area, they would stay at different places. At these places they would discuss politics at the dinner table or around the stove. It was a good way to develop a network of people who knew you and knew what you thought on issues. Ultimately it paid off at the ballot box." [16]

The ballot box was very kind to the Progressives in their first election that year. Over 140,000 signatures gathered put the party on the ballot statewide. During that election, LaFollette edged out Schmedeman - who hurt himself trying to get on the farmer's side by supporting a price-fixing measure for commodities supported by other Midwestern governors like Olson and Langer while at the same time supporting law and order measurers against striking dairy farmers and ensuring the nation's milk supply at the orders of the Roosevelt administration - by 373,093 votes to 359,467. LaFollette's feelings about the Republican Party seem to bear itself out as its nominee for governor, Howard Greene, had the party's worst showing in a gubernatorial election ever, finishing third with 172,980 votes.

Such support was mirrored in Polk County. The Progressives swept the county, winning all but two elections that were on the ballot. Finishing second was the Socialist Party and the GOP, the traditional party of the county, wound up a dismal fourth in most of the county-wide elections. Phil LaFollette grabbed 4,183 votes and brother Bob, also on the ballot, won 4,918 votes. In the *Leader*'s circulation area in next-door Burnett and Barron counties, the Progressives swept the elections there as well.

The Progressives may have had a popular political platform in Polk County in 1934, but the LaFollettes could have run on any party label that fall and won. There was a power in their name that transcended ideology and party label that even to this day still resonates with the voters (Douglas LaFollette, a relative, is the current Secretary of State). That power was based on the character and charisma of the patriarch who tried to give his own definition of progressivism when so many others had their own ideas.

Who's Progressivism?

From a political standpoint, Wisconsin is popularly seen as state where the politics are clean, high-minded and infused with a civic tradition and ethos. Where corruption, even of the pettiest kind, is frowned upon and citizens are actively engaged in government. But where do all these popular stereotypes come from? Politics in Wisconsin was no different than politics anywhere else from the end of the War Between the States through the Gilded Age. It took one man to create all those images that last even to this day for the most part.

The development of Wisconsin followed the railroads. Such railroads made it possible for the interior of the state away from the rivers (the Mississippi for example) and the lakes (like Michigan), the natural forms of transportation, to be developed and settled. The railroads were a part of the state's great lumber boom, made it easier to transport farm goods from market-to-market and made the development of heavy industry possible. Thus, those who ran the railroads had a powerful influence over who governed the state, which at that time meant control of the Republican Party, the dominant party in the Upper Midwest after the War Between the States. By the late 19th Century, control of the GOP fell to a railroad developer named John Spooner, along with a lumber baron, Philetus Sawyer. Both men were U.S. Senators and both men, along with their acolyte Henry Payne, chairman of the state's Republican Party, controlled the Wisconsin. The business of the state was indeed business and whatever needed to be done to smooth along such business, such as a slush fund of $300,000 maintained by the party off the interest from banks that held state monies, was done, no questions asked.[17]

Except that one person did ask questions, someone outside the business class. It would make for a great Hollywood story that a young Robert LaFollette, ala Jimmy Stewart in *Mr. Smith Goes to Washington*, would become so outraged when he was offered a bribe by Sawyer to influence a judge who happened to be a friend for a favorable outcome in a case, that it precipitated his break with the state's GOP leadership and led to his transformation into "Super Progressive, Scourge of Corrupt Politics!" Yes, LaFollette was ticked off that he was offered a bribe and soon promptly reported it publicly and soon became a pariah in state GOP circles.[18] But he was never a part of those circles to begin with and it never occurred to him that was how business was conducted in Wisconsin because he was not a businessman. He was intellectual, having been greatly influenced by friend Charles Van Hise, the then President of the University of Wisconsin, and by being a popular speaker on the Chautauqua circuit. [19] He was lawyer, elected Dane County District Attorney in 1880 and then a U.S. Congressman from 1884-1888. He lived an upper-middle class home in the Madison suburb of Maple Bluff, not in the mansions built by the industrialists. His wife didn't stay in the shadows but had an active career herself and was a suffragist.

LaFollette's campaign against the corruption that permeated throughout the state was the result of a struggle between class and culture more so than any personal affront. A new class of people had emerged, as always emerges in times of great economic expansion, to deal with the handling of the wealth, its creation and its effects upon the larger economy and society. It was this class that became the foundation of the progressive movement and the little submovements inside of it like prohibition or women's suffrage.

But it would take a lot more than persons of this class to take LaFollette to political power. He returned to politics in 1892 to try and capture the Republican Party away from the business class, but it took him eight years to do so up to his election as governor in 1900. This eight-year period was about the creation of alliances and coalitions of like interests and the stacking of particular state voting blocs that would eventually be the basis for the "progressive wing" of the GOP, the Progressive Party itself, and the modern Democratic Party.

One of the first partnerships he struck was with Nils Haugen, a Norwegian politician who LaFollette backed for governor in 1894. He also reached out to the state's farmers, who, like many farmers across the Upper Midwest, were angry at the rates they paid to ship their goods on the state's railroads, a fact LaFollette wasted no words to point out. He also made a play for the state's emerging dairy industry by supporting the effort to suppress the sale of oleomargarine in favor of natural butter. It wasn't before long that colored oleomargarine was banned and lard-white oleo was sold at a prohibitive 15 cent per pound tax. [20]

And while denouncing the state GOP machine, he slid up to a "cleaner" political machine the Socialists were putting together in the state's largest city of Milwaukee. By 1850, the city was 60 percent German and many of those were the "48ers" the freethinking refugees of the revolution of 1848. They were more than receptive to socialist ideas and organized themselves through newspapers, schools, militias and the *Turnerveinen* or "Turner Halls" that were German social clubs.[21] A school teacher named Victor Berger formed the Social Democratic Party in 1898, which also added the support of new Italian and Jewish immigrants from Eastern Europe that were coming to town by that time. In 1910, the SDP won the mayor's office in Milwaukee which they were to hold until 1960. They also elected 16 members to the 23-seat Common Council and Berger himself was elected to the U.S. House of Representatives that same year as well.[22] In 1912, Socialist Party presidential candidate Eugene Debs won 26 percent of Milwaukee's vote. But even with the Socialist takeover of Milwaukee, LaFollette wouldn't have lost either way. The people who the SPD were replacing in city politics were reform Republicans of the LaFollette stripe. There were also businessmen in the Cream City who, by 1900, were fed up with statewide corruption and wanted change. They backed and bankrolled LaFollette to provide such change. [23]

As LaFollette was stacking up voting blocs, he was also formulating the policies that he would ultimately enact as governor. These included open primaries, reform of the state's tax system, regulation of railroads, banks and insurance companies. Many of these policies were formulated on the very University of Wisconsin campus just a few miles down State St. from the capital and LaFollette invited the professors who created the formulas to take part in government. No longer would business and their agenda be in control and no longer were the hacks in charge handing out favors. The era of reform that first burst through the national consciousness beginning with the Populist campaign of 1892 had expanded itself from the farmers into the new classes and created the coalition that LaFollette and his allies would win elections on for nearly 50 years. The dislocations in society in the transition from an agricultural-based to an industrial-based economy, could be responsibly managed by progressivism, as its leaders believed.

Through sheer attrition and through divisions within the machine itself, LaFollette could no longer be denied his party's nomination for governor in 1900 as he was in 1896 and 1898.[24] He was re-elected twice and then moved to the U.S. Senate in 1905. He took his battles against the system to Washington and in a body that he referred to as "dead, old and rotten." [25] He used its tradition-bound rules to fight the same battles for reform instead of being burned out like so many reformers are after many encounters with raw power. His tenacity for reform inspired those on the other end of Capitol Hill, members of the U.S. House, to revolt against the leadership of Speaker Joe Cannon and dump him over the side in 1911.[26]

His status in Washington D.C. made him famous nationwide and made progressives and reformers see him as their champion.[27] When such a level of prestige is reached by any national politician, ultimately talk of running for president begins and so it was for LaFollette. The progressive reform of the intraparty primary made the once unthinkable now possible, directly challenging a sitting president of the United States from within one's own political party, something he intended to do against the unpopular incumbent in the White House, William Howard Taft. There was just one problem. Somebody else wanted to challenge Taft too.

Theodore Roosevelt had not lost interest in politics when he stepped aside from the presidency in favor of his good friend Taft in 1909. Roosevelt felt Taft had betrayed him and his polices during his time in office and was unable to stand-up to the party stalwarts. As soon as Roosevelt had returned from a tour of Europe in 1911, leading progressives sought out "Teddy" and successfully convinced him to run. Roosevelt would later claim that Taft had used political machine power to muscle him out of the GOP nomination, but Roosevelt and his allies did virtually the same thing to LaFollette that same year. LaFollette beat Taft and Roosevelt in both the Wisconsin and North Dakota primaries, but that gave him just 36 delegates at the GOP convention in Chicago that year.[28] Roosevelt sucked all the oxygen, all the structure and support the progressive movement could have given LaFollette and took it for himself. It opened up a split in the progressive movement that within eight years became a bloody chasm.

"They were too much like each other," progressive newspaper editor William Allen White said of LaFollette and Roosevelt and it's true both were energetic and ambitious.[29] But what both men thought progressivism was began to diverge by 1912. To LaFollette, it was a movement of political reform and social justice. Inequities in the great transition from farm to factory and the corruption it spawned would be straightened out. The famous picture of LaFollette standing on a hay wagon in a field in Polk County, fists clenched in fighting mode, reflected his view of progressivism.[30] Roosevelt, meanwhile, campaigned as the movie cameras rolled, reflecting his modern view of progressivism.[31] More so than just being from the East, Roosevelt's views resonated with those who weren't just interested anti-trust legislation or removing some hack politician from a county commission for corruption. It was about changing the nature of man itself so they would no longer accept such bribes or be so greedy. It led to beliefs that man could be made perfect or "progress" from his primal urges and lusts. This inevitably led to prohibition, to Americanism, to women's suffrage, vegetarianism and so forth. Taken to extremes, however, it also led to communism, fascism, eugenics and Nietzschian theories of "supermen." Roosevelt viewed himself as part of a global movement for such change of the established order. LaFollette's mindset never left that Polk County field. This difference was ultimately played out in coming cataclysm that would engulf progressive and populist politics and defined the independent parties of the Upper Midwest for years to come.

War and remembrance

In June 2004, more people remembered the 60th anniversary of D-Day, the invasion of Western Europe by the Allies in World War II on the 6th of the month than they did the 90th anniversary of the assassination of Austro-Hungarian archduke Franz Ferdinand on the 28th. And yet, without the latter there would not be the former. The tragedy of World War I that Ferdinand's death set off had enormous consequences all across the world, including the Upper Midwest. The war helped shaped the politics of the region for many years during its course and in its aftermath. It led to the downfall of some politicians and helped the fortunes of others. The disillusionment following the war helped the independent political parties of the region cement loyalties among different groups of voters. But the war that was eventually spawned from the "war to end all wars," ultimately led to the death of these parties, leaving them nothing but remembrance.

The United States leaned on its traditional neutrality when the war began, the tradition set forth by George Washington in his farewell address to avoid all foreign entanglements. But in a country with a good chunk of its population now foreign born or ancestored, with U.S. banks and financiers having investments all over the world, with U.S. companies trading in war supplies with both the Allies and Central Powers, sticking to this strict neutrality would become very difficult. Such a policy didn't keep people from choosing sides anyway. Those descended from the British Isles, with the exception of the Irish of course, supported Great Britain and America's debt to France for its support in the Revolution was not forgotten either, especially in the ranks of the *Lafayette Escadrille*, the group of volunteer American pilots who flew for France. But this was now counterbalanced by a large contingent of German-Americans, once previously divided by religion, ideology and the various regions of Germany from which they immigrated from, now united in backing the Second Reich. Numerous Irish-Americans had no desire to fight for the oppressors of their homeland, Great Britain. And Jews, newly immigrated from Russia and Eastern Europe, considered the Allied cause illegitimate because their side included the Russian Empire, the land of the pogroms which drove them from their homes. Such a balance of public opinion kept the U.S. out of the war for the first two and half years and it helped President Woodrow Wilson get re-elected in 1916, contrasting his support for American neutrality against that of Republicans like Theodore Roosevelt, who wanted the U.S. to get involved.

But Wilson was not diametrically opposed to war and forces outside of his control were pulling the country towards entering the conflict. Many of his fellow progressives, like Roosevelt, wanted to get the U.S, involved and formed preparedness committees, or private militias, to train young Americans for what they thought was the inevitable fight. With the military situation a stalemate in 1916-1917, Great Britain angled to get the U.S. involved. They had cut the underwater cables from Germany to the U.S., preventing German accounts of battles and other war news from reaching the U.S. public and leaving only Allied accounts and Allied propaganda to fill the ears and minds of many Americans.[32] Such reports, including bogus ones of German atrocities, turned American sentiment against Germany. The British blockade of Germany greatly increased the dependency of American banks and munitions makers on the Allies. But above all else it was the Germans use of unrestricted submarine warfare and sinking of the *Lusitania* that brought America into arms of the Allies. Although it would be many years later when it was learned that the British had used trans-Atlantic ocean liners to smuggle war supplies from the U.S., making them targets of the German submarine blockade, the immediate of the loss of life, especially 128 American citizen lives, simply reinforced what British propaganda had already been saying all along: the Germans were the modern-day Huns, the modern-day barbarians threatening all of Western civilization. [33]

That would have been news to German-Americans considering that theirs was one of the more enlightened nations in Western civilization. Germany led Europe in graduate education, education of the very young (kindergartens,of course, were a German idea) and the application of science to government. Some of the University of Wisconsin professors who traveled down State St. in Madison from the university to the state capitol at the invitation of Governor LaFollette were German in origin. German achievements in science, arts and letters were recognized around the world.[34] The barbarian argument for wasn't going to fly with LaFollette, now in the Senate and now in a position to decide the U.S. course into war. Sure, with a state population that was 20 percent German in origin, it would have been political suicide to advocate U.S. entry into the war on the side of the Allies, particularly when German-speaking counties across the Midwest had a habit of voting against pro-war politicians.[35] But he also saw what war would do to progressivism itself. It would exalt efficiency over democracy, put profits for bankers and munitions makers over relief for farmers or the unemployed, bend the Constitution out of shape by inflating the powers of the presidency, as wars often did, and lead to conscription as well. LaFollette simply saw no benefit to the U.S. by entering the war.[36]

Wilson's campaign slogan in 1916 was "He kept us out of war." But he felt that despite his campaign promises, if the Germans went back to unrestricted submarine warfare to starve the British into submission, it would mean war with the U.S. given the strong American ties to the Allies in commerce and finance and especially after the *Lusitania* incident. Of course the infamous Zimmerman telegram (where German foreign minister Alfred Zimmerman, in a private cable intercepted by British intelligence, promised Mexico territory in the southwestern United States if they allied themselves with Germany in the event of war between both countries) was the final touch. But if the U.S. was going to war, Wilson decided it was going to be a war on his terms, on progressive terms, not on notions of merely conquering land. The Allied cause would not be for conquering new colonies in Africa, but it would be to spread democracy, to give peoples the right of self determination, provide freedom of the seas and end the secret treaties and diplomacy that had become an unsavory part of European politics. [37] If progressivism could remake man, it could also remake the world and such sentiment became the basis of Wilson's 14 Points. It was the platform that became the Allied cause once the U.S. entered the war beginning with Wilson's State of Union Address in early April of 1917 where he asked the Congress to declare war on Germany. Ninety years later, so-called "neoconservatives," like long-lost grandchildren, claim the same mantle of progressivism and its belief in altering the make-up of man and his world as Roosevelt and Wilson once claimed and which LaFollette rejected.

It wasn't that LaFollette was opposed to such ideas, he simply felt they would be better pursued as a neutral rather than as an active participant. But given the fact that war supporters in Senate wouldn't allow LaFollette to speak by refusing him recognition on the Senate floor during the debate, it didn't matter what he thought anymore. The hysteria that gripped Europe two and half years before when the war began now gripped the United States.[38] And those who tried to stand in its way were mowed down like so many soldiers in France before the machine gun.

LaFollette was the first to receive the brunt of the war hysteria. He was one of six senators (the others were the NPL's Asle Gronna of North Dakota, Harry Lane of Oregon, William Stone of Missouri, George Norris of Nebraska and J.K. Vardaman of Mississippi) to vote against the war declaration. Most of them, like LaFollette himself, were from rural and small states with their lingering, frontier-like suspicions of the upper-class bias and manipulation, particularly to more populated and more modern big cities of the East.[39] By the same token, such men were not held in high regards in those very precincts. MIT students in Cambridge, Mass. burned

LaFollette in effigy, the pro-war *New York Times* called him and other antiwar congressmen "traitors," the Associated Press deliberately distorted a speech he made before the Non-Partisan League's convention in St. Paul to make it look like he defended the sinking of the *Lusitania* and a Columbia University professor called him a traitor and compared him to that infamous of all traitors, Judas Iscariot.[40] Yet the real betrayals came from old progressive friends like Former UW President Van Hise, who called his views "dangerous to the country." [41] Despite the fact that LaFollette approved most of the war measures that came before Congress that session except for the Espionage Act for its curtailment of civil liberties and the Conscription Act, he had to survive an expulsion attempt by some of his more disgruntled fellow senators. LaFollette's colleague from Wisconsin, Congressman Berger of Milwaukee, was not so fortunate. He was denied his seat in the House of Representatives not once, but twice in 1919 and 1921 for alleged pro-German sentiment.[42]

The *Times* had pointed out that many of the antiwar Congressmen came from German-speaking parts of the country, particularly the Upper Midwest. And yet the hysteria spread here too. Changing the names of certain foods, like French Fries into "Freedom Fries" because certain politicians didn't care for France's lack of support during Gulf War II, isn't a new thing because sauerkraut became "Liberty Cabbage" during the First World War. Anything and everything that had any kind of German origin or name or suffix was held in suspect and changed. Or, if it was a German language publication or institution like the *Turnerveinen*, it was closed down or suppressed. Even in solidly German Milwaukee. In 1916, over 30,000 students took German language classes in local Milwaukee schools. In just two years, that number shrunk to 400. The German-English Academy, a prominent secondary private school, changed its name to the Milwaukee Academy (it's now Milwaukee University School). The so-called Loyalty Legion was created to be on the look-out for pro-German traitors, real or imagined and Prohibition made its way into the Constitution that year partially due to the fact that it would hurt breweries owned by German families, including the Schlitzs, Pabsts, Millers and Blatzs, that called Milwaukee home and made it famous.[43]

"The right to control their own government according to constitutional forms is not one of the rights that the citizens of this country are called upon to surrender in a time of war." [44] LaFollette's view, however, was a minority one, even among progressives. And as he had predicted, the war had made progressivism bite itself and go mad. Dissent from the war hysteria was suppressed. Whether it was *The Masses* magazine being refused delivery by the U.S. Postal Service or Socialist Party presidential candidate Eugene V. Debs being thrown in jail when his opposition to the war was called sedition, or even the later Red Scare, progressive values of democracy, expertise and science in government in the name of the common good and abhorration of corruption were lost in the desire to save the world and save mankind. Those who pointed this out were attacked, smeared, ruined or put in jail.[45] This feeling manifested itself fully during the Minnesota gubernatorial election of 1918.

Charles Lindbergh Sr. was a progressive hero in 1911 when he was a part of the successful revolt against Speaker of the House Joe Cannon (Lindbergh credited LaFollette's influence for sparking the revolt.)[46] Throughout his career in Congress from 1907-1917, Lindbergh specialized in the study of money and its misuses from both the private sector (the money trust) and the public (the Federal Reserve Bank). Such interests were a reflection of the Sixth Congressional District which he represented that extended from its base in heavily German Stearns County through the Swedish populated areas around Lindbergh's home in Little Falls north all the way to the Canadian border (today, reflecting the population trends in the state, the sixth includes Stearns but extends southeast to include the exurban areas around the northwest, north and east sides of the Twin Cities metropolis.) This rural area had plenty of farmers wondering why they were always constantly squeezed financially by the powers that be.[47] Such reform politics ran in Lindbergh's blood as his father, Ola Mansson, was part of the liberal faction in the Riksdag, the Swedish parliament.[48] Like father, like son as Lindbergh was a prominent member of the progressive wing of the state's GOP and got help from the national Progressive Republican League throughout his career. In 1918 he was the Non-Partisan League's candidate in the GOP primary against incumbent governor J.A.A. Burquist as the league spread quickly from neighboring North Dakota to have 25,000 members in the Gopher State.[49]

Lindbergh's views on the war were perfectly consistent with his monetary views. He believed that the war was being fought in the name of the moneyed interests and the war munitions makers and that American boys should not be dying to make a few people rich. His opponents didn't view it that way. Infected with the war hysteria, they used the state's Committee on Public Safety—an organization set up to direct the state's war effort that quickly became a rhetorical lynching party against opponents of the war—to tar and feather (or at least effigies of him were) Lindbergh in many Minnesota towns before being hung from lamp posts.[50] Besides being called pro-German, Lindbergh was also supposedly tied in with the Communists too when the IWW unions of the Iron Range backed him and in response to the NPL's public ownership platform. He was called an anti-Catholic bigot to boot.[51] Many towns in southern Minnesota refused to have Lindbergh campaign in them as the heavily German region descended to a state of near internal warfare between pro and antiwar opponents.[52]

Americanism was one of the progressive sub-movements of the early 20th century that was determined to purge the ethnic identity and background of immigrant children through the expanded public school system. It would replace that identity with "pure" American values and ideas which, ironically, was similar in intent if not method of Czarist bureaucrats engaged in "Russification" of the diverse peoples of the Russian Empire. This movement reached its height during the war. Now cast in patriotic tones in its effort to try and stamp out potential fifth column populations, forced assimilation not only affected German-speaking areas, but Scandinavian as well. Lindbergh had to know his campaign was in trouble when the popular Swedish-American newspaper *Svenska Amerikanska* attacked him in editorials.[53] The war had divided Scandinavian populations between assimilists and those who wished keep their ethnic identification. The hysteria had frightened these populations even though Scandinavian nations were not even involved in the war. Thus, the Norwegian Lutheran Church changed its name to United Lutheran and then to today's Evangelical Lutheran Church. Such assimilation moves were opposed by persons like the famed novelist Ole Rolvaag but to no avail. War forces people to choose sides and when sides become "loyalists vs. disloyalists," when the terms become "for us or against us," or even more stark "be like us or else!" then it's much easier to get people to fall into line as they did against Lindbergh. Burquist won the primary with 199,325 votes to Lindbergh's 150,626. Arthur C. Townley summed up the situation nicely when he said "We are against this goddamn war but can't afford to advertise it,"[54] as he tried in vain and at the point of splitting the NPL to keep the war from being an issue in the campaign.

While Lindbergh's career was doomed by his defeat, the causes he held forth were not. The term *hubris* is from the Greek meaning overweening pride and insolence that often times brings back "divine" retribution. For the Rooseveltian and Wilsonian progressives, their retribution came in the form of the Versailles Treaty. LaFollette regained his political footing by attacking the treaty in the Senate and in the pages of his new magazine, *The Progressive*. Joined in coalition by other Midwestern and Western progressives like Hiram Johnson of California and William Borah of Idaho and Eastern conservatives like Henry Cabot Lodge, the treaty went down to defeat. That this happened was due in large part to the disillusionment felt in the aftermath of the war. America's involvement in the war, although decisive for the Allied cause, lasted only a year and a half. It was hardly enough time to change traditional American attitudes on foreign entanglements and alliances that the treaty threatened to alter. The fact that U.S. troops were still deployed in Russia despite the end of the conflict made people fear of continuing warfare, troop deployments and conscription. The immediate aftermath of the war, the turmoil it caused throughout the world and the spread of the Spanish Influenza disease that millions suffered and died from because of troop movements, destroyed progressive images of a golden age. Add on top of that the daily bureaucratic interference in terms of wartime price controls, food rationing, (with resulting inflation when those price controls were eventually lifted) and a collapse in farm prices, led to a rejection of progressive ideals at the ballot box. The GOP swept the Wilsonians out of power in 1920, replacing him with the very kind of hack politician in Warren G. Harding they so abhorred. LaFollette, meanwhile, told an audience at a packed state Assembly chamber on March 25, 1921 that he "would not change my record on the war for that of any man, living or dead," and received a standing ovation.[55]

Opposing the war did not necessarily mean political death and in fact may very well have helped in the success of the independent third parties of the Upper Midwest during the early to mid-1930s. Four years after nearly being expelled from the Senate, LaFollette won re-election easily and ran a credible third-party candidacy for the White House in 1924 that finished second in many parts of the country.[56] After being torn apart by the war, the Non-Partisan League was able to rebuild around the loyalties gained from the *Volksdeutschen* of North Dakota for William Langer's opposition to the war. Likewise, LaFollette was able to cement the support of Germans in Wisconsin to his campaigns and bequeath them to his sons in following campaigns. The succeeding decades were all about peace, whether it was Washington Naval Disarmament Conference or the Kellogg-Briand Pact to outlaw war as a means of settling disputes among nations. The shabby treatment World War I veterans received in the early part of the Depression by the Hoover Administration (being driven out of their shacks they set up along the Anacostia River in Washington D.C. by the Army) enforced the mood that the war was a tragic mistake altogether. And what furthered this feeling even more, cause even outrage in fact, was the findings of the Nye Committee

North Dakota's Gerald P. Nye was barely in Senate before he was approached by the Women's International League for Peace and Freedom to investigate the international munitions industry in 1933. An investigating committee was eventually formed in the spring 1934 which he headed and the reports the committee gave, mostly written by *New Republic* writer John T. Flynn, who would go on to be a strong supporter the America First Committee before World War II, outraged many. What these reports showed was a strong link between the American government's entry into the war and the lobbying of the munitions industry and the lobbying of the nation's banks with all their war loans made to the Allies. Nye stated clearly in a 1936 speech that "the record of facts makes it altogether fair to say that these bankers were in the heart and center of a system that made our going to war inevitable." Nye referred to such industrialists and bankers as "merchants of death." Such anti-corporatist sentiment was in perfect line with early progressive sentiment although it also showed a clear shift to the left in the movement now centered in the Upper Midwest (Alger Hiss was the chief legal counsel to the Nye Committee). Indeed, LaFollette's Progressive Party presidential candidacy was endorsed by the Socialist Party as both party platforms began to look more and more alike after the Progressive split because of the war.[57]

The Wilsonian-Roosevelt progressives, however, didn't go away despite their failures. They entrenched themselves in both parties, showing their power, wealth and influence in the 1940 election when internationalists like Franklin Roosevelt and Wendell Willkie were the Democratic and Republican party nominees for president respectively. The isolationism of the independent third parties began to lose its appeal to voting blocs of ethnic Poles, Norwegians, Danes, Dutch, South Slavs, Greeks, Belgians and French when their nations found themselves conquered and brutally repressed by the Nazis as World War II got underway.[58] Then the leftists lost their hatred of munitions makers when their ideological masters in the Soviet Union came under attack by Hitler's forces and demanded that the "merchants of death" now go to work for them. Even the short Russo-Finnish War of 1939-1940 played a role in splitting the independent political parties of the Upper Midwest. When some Farm-Labor officials, especially those close to the communists, defended the Soviet's right to invade Finland and called it a "liberation," many Minnesota Finns demanded that they be purged from the party, furthering the split within the F-L during its time of troubles in the aftermath of the 1938 election. [59]

Isolationism began to be seen as a cause of the right and lost its populist appeal, although the America First Committee included many a diverse ideology. Its strength in late 1941 was over 800,000 and had Lindbergh's famous son was now speaking out against American involvement in the war. But America First was financed not just by membership dues, but also by prominent contributions from American industrialists and businessmen like Robert Wood, its President, who was the head of Sears-Roebuck; William Regnery, who's son would later found Regnery Publishing; H. Smith Richardson of the Vicks Chemical Corporation and its founder Stuart Douglas Jr., son of a vice-president in the Quaker Oats Corporation.[60] Lindbergh's unfortunate comments about British and Jewish attempts to drag the United States into the war revived all the pro-German (and this time pro-Nazi) attacks against opponents of the war. By the time Japanese bombers flew over Pearl Harbor on the dawn of

Dec. 7, the antiwar ideology of the independent political parties of the Upper Midwest was already losing its hold on the electorate. When those Japanese Zeroes finished their bombing runs, that hold, outside of the German and Irish communities, was gone and isolationism became a dirty word in American politics.

Kevin Phillips called the period between 1890 and the World Wars the "lesser cousins' war," the struggle between Anglo and Germanic America to see which European power the U.S. would point to. In reality, the war was over before long before the both countries squared off on the battlefields of France and Belgium. Most German and Scandinavian politicians spoke English while in government and in their speeches before legislative bodies. No one seriously suggested any changes in or upon the hundreds of years of British law and tradition that guided the U.S. government and its politics in favor of Germanic or Nordic governing traditions. While the pro vs. antiwar struggle tore the country apart during the First World War, there was no such turmoil in the second. No one outside of a few hardcore Bundists (some of whom trained at Camp Hindenburg near Grafton, Wisconsin) wanted to be on Hitler's side. By World War II, the U.S. military even had ethnic German leaders such as Eisenhower and Nimitz. Despite there being over 15 million ethnic Germans in *Mittel Amerika*, they gave their lives and support to the government of Anglosphere.[61] Pretty soon they would be giving their support to the political parties of that government, the Republicans and Democrats.

Sliding towards history

LaFollette's two sons, Phillip and Robert Jr., cut their teeth politically on their father's 1924 presidential campaign.[62] As an independent campaign, LaFollette's was one of the best, gaining 16.5 percent of the vote, finishing second in 11 northern and western states and winning Wisconsin on top of it. LaFollette Jr. took over his father's senate seat in 1925 upon the latter's death but came close to leaving politics altogether by 1929, tired of living in his famous father's shadow.[63] Yet the Great Depression galvanized both men back into the arena and galvanized the voting blocs and coalitions that their father successfully put together 30 years before.

Phil LaFollette led a successful revolt within the GOP against incumbent governor Walter Kohler Sr., ousting him in the primary and winning the fall general election. After being turned out by the Republicans in 1932, he finally declared his independence from what was believed to be a dying party in 1934 with his formation of the Progressive Party with his brother and himself heading the ticket. Not only did the brothers win, Phillip for governor and Robert Jr. for the Senate, but scores of Progressive congressmen and state senators and assemblymen were also elected on their ticket. They believed they upheld their father's legacy and continued it locally with regulations on chain banks and retail stores, shifting the tax burden from property to income, unemployment insurance and road building. Much of this agenda was similar to that of the New Deal and for a time the LaFollettes and FDR were on good terms in the same way Floyd B. Olson was. LaFollette hoped to bring progressive Democrats into his tent as well with FDR's endorsement as that endorsement did for Olson's Farm-Labor Party. But, for the second time in 20 years, another Roosevelt would frustrate the ambitions of the LaFollettes.

Phil LaFollette believed in government like any progressive, but also believed in community to keep such government responsive to the needs of the people. The National Recovery Administration, however, violated those beliefs. The controversial NRA, with its blue eagle symbol, allowed for monopoly pricing among various industries that were its members. The close cooperation between government and industry was in direct conflict with the progressives' communitarian philosophy and LaFollette criticized it.[64] That still didn't stop the governor from supporting Roosevelt again in 1936 and using his overwhelming popularity to help the Progressives sweep the election statewide that year. But if one looked at the results closely, one could see that Roosevelt was digging the LaFollettes' political grave. The very coalition his father tried to build to get elected was now the governing coalition of the Democratic Party, which became the nation's governing party. The Progressive Party was a gamble, based on the hope that the GOP and the national Democratic parties would remain unpopular with local voters. As Roosevelt carried Wisconsin three times and Truman once, that popularity was bound to trickle down and threatened the Progressives. Phil LaFollette acknowledged "For the first time in nearly two decades the great mass of people has become the Democratic Party, enhancing it as the only available instrument for change and progress." [65]

Thus the collision course was set and finally came into the open by 1938. LaFollette was clearly opposed to the president's court-packing scheme, adding more members to the Supreme Court, as unconstitutional. He came to believe that the New Deal, with its emphasis on centralization and collectivism, was incompatible with progressivism and wanted to take his Progressive Party national as an alternative. "Men can still have work and still be free," [66] was its slogan. This was done despite the fact Robert Jr. was a loyal supporter of FDR in the Senate and even supported the court-packing scheme.[67] But in the interest of family unity, Robert Jr. agreed to go along with National Progressives of America party despite his private opposition. But he did not show up for the party's first rally in Madison and smartly so. The massed rally at the Stock Pavilion on the University of Wisconsin-Madison campus, complete with its spotlights, dark backgrounds, loud speakers and banners with the new party symbol of an "X" in a red circle with a white background, was immediately criticized as "fascistic," fair or not. In any case, such a rally was a far cry from campaigning from a hay wagon in Polk County and the negative spin from it just added to Phillip LaFollette's problems, like splits within the party over the unionization of food processing plants which many farmers opposed. The reforms passed by the legislature that greatly increased the governor's power (Wisconsin has one of the most powerful governor's offices in the nation) and the high-handed way he fired University of Wisconsin president R.Glenn Frank, gave such charges of "fascism" a credibility they would have otherwise lacked.[68] The NPA was able to run a few candidates in Iowa and California to go with all the Progressive office holders in Wisconsin, but they were all whipped in the GOP landslide of that year, including LaFollette, who fell in the governor's race to Julius Peter Heil 543,675 votes to 353,381.

The Progressives were the only independent party of the Upper Midwest that tried to become a national party on its very own (the NPL was importing a tactic to other states, not a separate political party). Yet the middle and upper middle classes that progressivism depended upon were wiped out or impoverished by the Great Depression and would not recover until after World War II. Farmers too, drifted back to their traditional home in the GOP or were following Farmer's Union members into the Democratic Party to be with the party of Roosevelt and the New Deal that aided them just as they did in North Dakota. Wisconsin was also changing demographically to become more of an urban and industrial state. LaFollette's Progressives rejected the class based and union politics of neighboring Minnesota's Farm-Labor Party. But such groups would be the future building blocs of Wisconsin politics and the Democrats would be the ones in position to build on them.

LaFollette's loss did not mean the end of the Progressive Party. Robert Jr. won re-election under that banner in 1940 and Orland Loomis won the governor's office again for the Progressives in 1942. But such success was fleeting. Loomis died before taking office, leaving the governor's chair to be occupied once gain by a Republican, lieutenant governor Walter Goodland. The Progressives won only 76,000 votes in the 1944 election for governor while former Milwaukee mayor and socialist Daniel

Hoan, gained 536,357 votes on the Democratic ticket that year, the most votes for a Democrat since Schmedeman in 1932. The trend against the Progressives began just as World War II was at its height and it was not a coincidence.

Let's go back to Polk County in 1944 and see what makes the front pages of the *Inter-County Leader*. The local co-op meeting minutes are still there along with the co-op ads. There are still some items on the National Farmer's Union activities. But they no longer commanded the front or even first few pages of the publication. Instead, it's all about the war. The war, the war and nothing but the war. Stories on various battles and theaters of the war got the large-point headlines along with news of a new blood drive or scrap drive to help our forces in the field. Within a decade the tone of the newspaper had completely changed. The burning news of the day was the existence of slot machines in local taverns, not on any milk strike or protest of low commodities prices. There certainly were no columns attacking the Federal Reserve or the Roosevelt administration either. In political news, one found the *Leader* endorsing the Democratic ticket of Roosevelt and Truman on its editorial page or saw stories on local Progressive party officeholders switching to the GOP. The only Progressive Party stories one might find were those where one official is saying the party should merge with the Republicans or the Democrats. One could read a story talking about the walkout staged by CIO union officials of the party's convention that year.[69]

Such walkouts and switches occurred because LaFollette Jr. stubbornly clung to his father's views of war in general and its warping affects upon government and the general populace. He voted against aid to France and Britain, was against conscription and against Lend-Lease. "Modern war poisons democracy," he said.[70] But in the *Leader* of 1944, such views would be blaspheme. The paper's support for the war was absolute and supporting the war meant supporting the President which meant supporting his party. Without Polk County, which often times chafed at the Madison-based leadership of the Progressives, there was no statewide Progressive Party.⁷¹ One only had to look at the 1940 election results that showed that if even the internationalist Wendell Willkie was winning the county, LaFollette's views were on the wane. But he would entertain no such merger with the war party no matter what. Simple reality, however, led him back to the GOP by 1946, after a vote of 284-128 in a statewide convention.⁷² Unless the Progressive Party, which won just six percent of the vote statewide two-years before, merged with someone or something sometime soon it would cease to be a story at all in the pages of the *Leader*, let alone any other newspaper or publication across the state.

But LaFollette was not welcomed back into the Republican Party like the Prodigal Son. Being absent from the GOP leadership and rank and file for over a decade did not make him a beloved figure. Many of his fellow Progressives did not follow him, deciding instead to join the Democrats. He also was spending less and less time in the state, bored and indifferent with the political scene there while focusing his attention upon government reorganization. He was vulnerable to an intra-party challenge and that came from an Outagamie County circuit judge named Joseph P. McCarthy, from Appleton.

McCarthy was not a figure with statewide stature, but he did have stature with two important voting blocs, Irish and German Catholics. Once again they were traumatized in being forced to join a cause with allies they were opposed to, the British Empire and the Soviet Union. McCarthy, a war veteran himself, appealed to their sentiment by saying that Stalin was just as bad as Hitler if not worse, and what was anyone doing to stop him, especially as he was enslaving their Catholic brothers in Eastern Europe?⁷³ Such sentiment he took with him to the peak of power by 1953 by being a scourge of communists nationwide (although fighting communism to McCarthy was fighting it at home, not abroad which showed a traditional Wisconsin isolationism still tinged his thinking) but in 1946 he was telling voters to "Send a Tail Gunner to Congress" while an absent LaFollette said nothing. The voters did exactly as McCarthy had asked and the Progressive Party, or even faction of it, had truly slid towards history. Afterwards, tragically, LaFollette took his own life in 1953, a forgotten man outside of Washington. He had spent his time since his defeat being a lobbyist for the very corporations his father and he himself once despised.[74]

The Nov. 4, 1948 edition of the *Leader* contained this story about a local boy making good:

"...Attorney Gaylord Nelson, son of Dr. and Mrs. A.N. Nelson of Clear Lake, defeated State Senator Fred Risser Sr., veteran Dane County Republican, for re-election in the Nov. 2 election. Nelson, the Democratic candidate, received 30,338 votes to 28,736 for Risser.

Mr. Nelson is a newcomer in Dane County politics and his feat is all the more notable because of his success against the veteran Risser in a historically Republican county. Mr. Nelson has been practicing law in Madison for two years. It is believed his principals and active, forthright campaign brought him victory over his opponent.

Incidentally, Dr. A.N. Nelson has been one of Polk County's leading Progressives for many years.

It is apparent that Gaylord, along with thousands of other Progressives, has concluded that the Democratic Party is the channel through which Progressives must work in order to put liberal thought and principles into effect."

So much change from just that one election. Nelson went on from the State Senate to the governor's office and then on to the U.S. Senate, becoming one of the founders of Wisconsin's modern Democratic Party. Dane County made its transition from Progressive Republican to Democratic stronghold. Risser's son Fred Jr., is a veteran Democratic state senator representing the same Madison district.

Even Polk County itself changed, although starting a bit later in the late 1980s. The loss of family farms, small town industrial jobs and businesses and the loss of ethnic identity and cohesion changed the all voting blocs around like a blackjack dealer shuffles a deck of cards. Newcomers, retirees from the Twin Cities, Milwaukee and Chicago, bought homes on county's lakes or cabins in the woods and hated the high taxes on their valuable property. They formed a conservative bloc with active Christian voters in Assembly of God and conservative Lutheran and Catholic churches that's elected Republicans to the county's state Assembly and Senate districts and carried the county for George W. Bush in the 2004 election. Likewise, artists, aging hippies and environmentalists migrated to the county about this time and formed a vibrant Green Party here. One can read until one can virtually feel the sharp differences of opinion in the editorial pages of the *Leader* and among its columnists.

But it's all a part of change that comes naturally within political, cultural, demographic and economic cycles. Such changes ushered in the Progressive Era in Wisconsin politics and such changes ushered it out as well. Voting patterns and cultural mindsets can last for generations, but ultimately they change because of forces beyond one person's control shuffle the deck so to speak and changed the hands that politicians play. But play they do and continue to do so until one of them figures it all out and calls that hand to victory.

Chapter 6—Back to the Future

"...A free state might show the rest of the world what can be done ... Let's think seriously about this."[6]

Author Claire Wolfe gave this statement as her endorsement for the objectives of the Free State Project (FSP) on their website. She and many others are taking the FSP seriously (in comparison to the harebrained projects that some Libertarians have engaged in the past to create their own countries on uninhabited islands) because they see its agenda—a goal of 20,000 persons who sign up to all move to New Hampshire and become activists for either libertarian and other forms decentralized politics—as no less crazier and in fact more feasible than it is for the Libertarian Party to elect a president of the United States.

The results of the 2004 election showed continued decline for traditional "third" (non-major) party politics. Among the largest of nation's non-major parties, all but one showed a decline of their voting percentages. The Libertarian ticket, led by Presidential candidate Michael Badnarik won only an estimated 381,000 votes, [7]down at least 5,000 from 2000's results, which is perhaps not all that bad considering

Badnarik's tax problems (he doesn't pay them, nor does he has a driver's license) never became fodder for the mainstream media.[2] Likewise, the Greens saw the biggest decline of all parties running candidates for president in their vote totals, a whopping 82 percent. The Green standard bearer David Cobb gained only 105,590 votes, way behind 2000 Green nominee Ralph Nader's 2,834,410 votes. Nader himself, running as an independent and as the candidate of the remnants of the Reform Party, hardly matched his vote total from 2000 as he gained just 397,468 votes. The only party that did better in 2004 from 2000 was the Constitution Party. The Michael Peroutka-led ticket had 135,260 votes, a 34 percent increase above 2000's 107,278 votes for Howard Phillips. Although they've increased their national vote totals since their party came into existence in 1992, even they have to be disappointed that they could not tap more into the near half-million votes Pat Buchanan gained as the Reform Party nominee back in 2000 or even reach their previous high of 185,000 back in 1996.

Utter defeat or disappointment has a way of showing one the truth of their situation. Some people or groups respond better to this truth than others. Unfortunately for many non-major party adherents, defeat after defeat has not revealed any such truth to them (like Harry Browne for example). So much so that not even a whack upside the head with 2x4 can make them see the reality that faces them: They will never replace either of the major parties in the U.S.' political milieu and they will never gain the footing of a "third" major party to go alongside the Democrats and Republicans.

"The results of 2004 were nothing but a rerun of 2000," Jason Sorens, the Yale graduate student and lecturer who founded the FSP said. "You can't expect significant change from that in the future. I think the leadership of the LP is more concerned about just keeping the whole organization afloat at this point than electing anybody or growing the party."[8]

Indeed for all parties, not just the LP, the period after any presidential or midterm election is always the most difficult because the attention and activism of such campaigns goes away and all that's left is debt and indifference, in other words "keeping the organization afloat" is just about all these parties can do at this juncture. Party leaders should be at least be given credit for that.

While they try to survive, perhaps they can also retool themselves with new strategies and new structures that can allow them to play their proper roles in U.S. politics. Maybe they can even take advantage of the potential new forces shaping those politics. And they can also realize why their current course is doomed to even more failure.

The truth is not always a pleasant thing

The litany of reasons as to why such non-major parties will not be competitive was touched upon in Chapter 2. Besides not being able to match the two majors in ballot access, they are not able to match them in terms of money and media coverage either. Beyond those technical reasons, the basic reality is the major parties have the voting loyalty of large cultural and economic blocs of voters throughout the country and the non-majors do not. And that loyalty is reinforced by the existing culture of the two-party system and ingrained voting habits that can last for generations.

That's why even efforts by a multi-billionaire like Ross Perot, or a celebrity candidate like Jesse Ventura, or even that of established and well-known politicians like Lowell Weicker in Connecticut or Walter Hickel in Alaska, has not changed the status quo. The long-term voting bloc loyalties to the major parties, either one or the other or both in some cases, outlasts the burst of unsettling energy that third parties provide the political scene. Like a tornado that tears through the countryside, the dust eventually settles, reconstruction begins and life goes on back to usual.

Bursts of energy exactly describe periods of third party success and influence in the country. Such periods take place usually at times of economic distress or social unrest when voters drop their major party loyalties when it is felt that they are not dealing with the problems of nation (or in fact are a cause of them). Such periods include 1831-1840 (the height of the Anti-Masonic Party and how it was a part of the formation of the Whig Party to rival Andrew Jackson's Democrats), 1844-1860 (the heyday of anti-slavery third parties Liberty and Free Soil that helped to destroy the Whigs; the struggle between the American (Know-Nothing) and Republican parties to see who would rival the Democrats); 1880-1892 (the Greenback and Populist parties that were ultimately swallowed up by the Democrats), 1912 (Roosevelt's Bull Moose Party and the high-water mark of the Socialist Party), 1932-1940 (the alternatives to the New Deal such as the Socialists, Communists and Union Party along with the strong leftist regional parties in the Upper Midwest and New York.) 1968-1980 (the spin offs from the conservative movement: The Libertarian, New York Conservative and American Independent parties) to the most recent such burst of third party activity from 1990-2000 (the revolt against major party corruption and globalization).

These periods have altered U.S. history, even in the smallest of ways. The major parties study the disruptions caused by such non-major parties and react accordingly. They absorb elements of these parties' platforms, issues and voting blocs into themselves. The whole Social Security program was Franklin Roosevelt's way to blunt the influence of leftist third parties as well as Huey Long,[4] (who FDR viewed as his most dangerous rival in 1936, not the Republicans.) Likewise, Ronald Reagan, by 1980, had incorporated into his campaign all the complaints against big government that George Wallace's AIP and the Libertarians had been saying since their founding in the late 1960s and early 1970s and used them to get elected.

The majors' ability to do this is another factor that dooms any non-major party's flights of fancy and dreams of major party status. Many of those associated with the non-majors want to believe they can be like the Republicans, a "third" party that made it big. This completely misreads the story of the rise of the GOP. The Republicans were formed in the disintegration of the Whig Party, not as a separate entity from it. Many leading Republicans, particularly in the northern parts of the country, were former Whigs (Abraham Lincoln, William Seward, Horace Greeley, Thurlow Weed) joined in alliance with anti-slavery Democrats, Free Soilers (who were also ex-Democrats) and anti-slavery members of the American (Know-Nothing) Party. Powerful business, religious and ethnic interests also played a part in its formation. Such disintegration could happen again to either the Democrats or Republicans in this day and age, but in the vacuum of that taking place, a new party would more than likely emerge from the remnants of the majors not from a non-major party superseding it.

Now that the latest period of non-major party activity has passed, it is a perfect time for non-major parties and those activists outside the two majors to truly assess where they stand in the nation's political pecking order and what they can accomplish with their limited resources. If it is to be the fate of the non-majors to only be really be effective at the margins of politics or away from the major centers power in the country, so be it. Such realism and pragmatism is would actually do the non-majors a great deal of good after wasted years of utopianism. But it does not mean such parties or political groups cannot have an impact, because history has shown again and again that they can have influence over the trends in American politics and behaviors of the major parties. If this is the role the non-major parties are to play, so be it as well. Somebody has to play Shylock or there is no *Merchant of Venice*

But only though developing different political tactics and only through developing cultural, ideological, regional and economic bases in some combination can such parties hope to be effective in this environment. This has been proven again and again throughout history. Several different independent political groups and parties know this as well and embarked on courses that may well make them the most effective, successful and influential non-major political groups in the coming future.

Regional broadcasts (League of the South, Free State Project and Second Vermont Republic)

Dr. J. Michael Hill does not particularly like politics. In fact, one might say he views it the same way a lot of Americans who are not political junkies do: A necessary evil comparable to taking out the garbage or doing the laundry. So when Southern academics such as himself got together with veteran regional political operatives in 1999 to try and form the Southern Party, the results, were, to be charitable, disastrous.

"We had people who didn't know what they were doing mixing with people who did. Our efforts were beset with a lot of infighting and personality conflicts that made it hard to get the Southern Party off the ground and led to a split in our ranks," Dr. Hill said. "But needless to say, even if we were successful, there are so many i's to dot in forming a new political party that it's almost not practical to do. Ballot access in the South is very difficult to obtain on top of trying to raise money and find candidates to run for public office." [5]

But the larger point Dr. Hill raised was that along with the routine difficulties non-major parties face in organizing, trying to form a centralized political structure clashed with the ideals of the group Dr. Hill leads, the League of the South (LOS).

The LOS—the name was changed from The Southern League as to not cause confusion with the minor league baseball association of the same name—is a Southern cultural organization that was formed in 1994 in Tuscaloosa, Alabama in order to promote the independence of the South "by all honorable means." By promoting Southern independence, what the LOS means is promoting the ideas of the Southern Confederacy as the South's law giving body along with preserving and promoting Southern culture (the LOS has already declared "cultural" independence from the United States during a ceremony in Montgomery, Alabama back when the group was founded in 1994). Such ideals conflicted with forming a centralized political organization like the SP almost from the start as Dr. Hill noted. He realized that in their zeal to start a political wing of their movement, they forgot their basic tenants.

"I do believe there is a Southern way to do things when it comes to politics," Dr. Hill said. "In the South, the individual candidate and the organization that surrounds him and his personality is more important than the party. The South votes the man and not so much the party and I think that's especially true in local races. For a long time the Democrats held the lock on the loyalty of Southern voters, but as we all know the Republicans have stolen the key. But as hard as it may seem to believe at this time in politics, most of the local elected officials around where I live in northwest Alabama are still all Democrats as by tradition."

The Democrats were so dominant in the South for so long that centralized party structures were not formed because they were not needed, leaving Southern politics decentralized and personality-driven. Former Alabama governor George Wallace is the best example of this kind of style. So to stay up with that tradition, the LOS simply eschewed the whole "Southern Party" idea and became an umbrella group for local and statewide political organizations and LOS chapters throughout the South that conduct a variety of grassroots political activities to further their cause.

"It's what we should have done right from the beginning," Dr. Hill lamented. "This way allows us the flexibility that we wouldn't have had trying to run our own party. We concentrate on the candidate and we support those whose principles don't conflict with ours."

Yet despite the loss of the time, LOS affiliated groups have made their impact felt. Just ask former, the stress being placed on the word "former," governors like David Beasley of South Carolina, Roy Barnes of Georgia and Bob Holden of Missouri. They ran afoul of League members and supporters for trying to replace symbols of the Confederacy, such as the Confederate flag, from either public places, like the South Carolina state capital, or on public symbols, like the Georgia state flag. Beasley's and Barnes' once promising careers were ruined in part by so-called "flaggers," Confederate flag supporters who picketed or made their presence felt at events the two men attended. Such moves highlighted these governors' opposition to the flag (or in the case of the opportunistic Beasley, his flip-flops) and helped to spark their defeat at the polls. Besides "flaggings," such affiliated LOS groups also endorse, or in some cases work with, candidates for local and statewide offices regardless of party that share their views. One of the LOS' biggest victories in the last national election was that of Tom Parker to the Alabama Supreme Court in which Parker upset a GOP incumbent in the party primary with local Southern heritage groups being the only organized support he had. There's no doubt someone like former Alabama Supreme Court Chief Justice Roy Moore will view such results as proof positive he can take on the state's GOP establishment that helped to remove him from office (led by current Governor Ed Reilly) and, backed by the same groups, be just as successful. Indeed, such a primary could be the nation's most talked about election in 2006.

"Generally speaking, the biggest success we've had is grassroots organizing down to the county level," Dr. Hill said. "We're moving toward having county-by-county chapters and we have high caliber people at those levels. But beyond the political level, the fact that the ideas of decentralization and secession have now become mainstream ideas across the county instead of just 'Southern' ideas is very gratifying. I think we've made an impact in making such ideas mainstream both politically and culturally."

Such regional politics could very well save Democratic Party from a permanent minority status in the South. In 1975, the Republican Party of Minnesota began to call themselves Independent Republicans or "IRs" in the wake of the Watergate scandal which had made the Republican label an unpopular (they dropped the "Independent" label in 1995.) Could not Southern Democrats do the same now that their party label has become poisonous to many voters in the South? Once upon a time the Southern Democrats, or "Dixiecrats" to use a more popular label, used to identify their party with rooster instead of a donkey. That tradition of independence could serve them well again. The Democrat mayor of Shelbyville, Kentucky, Tom Hardesty, said just as much in response to several local officials in his county switching parties late in 2004. "We're Democrats but we're conservative," Hardesty said in a story in Shelbyville Sentinel-News. "At the local level we need to pull away from the national party. The party has gone away from the principles of the 1930s and 1940s when it was dominant in America." [6]

That's talk Hill can support.

"I haven't heard it talked about publicly, yet privately some elected officials are styling themselves as 'Jeffersonian Democrats.' " Hill said. "Certainly this would be a change the LOS would support in terms of promoting Southern regionalism."

To get people to think regionally and locally, one needs an organization to do so. That's why the LOS' next project is not a political one but a cultural one. The Southern National Congress held its first meeting in March of 2005 after electing delegates in late 2004. Dr. Hill envisions it as activist body speaking out on Southern issues and trying to change the mindset of the region from being one of the most loyal and patriotic to the United States and the central government in Washington D.C. in a knee-jerk fashion, to one that once again sees itself as a distinctive place and people.

"The Southern National Congress is not a political party or structure in those terms, but will be a group of delegates who represent their own respective states and will speak out on the Southern issues," Hill said. "It's an ambitious project with a small beginning that I hope can provide a forum for a variety of Southerners from all walks of life in business, religion, politics, culture, academia to discuss and come to consensus on the issues facing the South."

Many see the South as the land of "secession" from the Union and "rebellion" against the United States. Yet such ideals did not originate from there. From Dec. 14, 1815 to Jan. 4 1815, a group of New Englanders met in Hartford, Connecticut to talk seriously of leaving the union after the War of 1812 began. These mostly New England merchants, whose sympathies in the war lie with Great Britain along with their commerce, were furious that the country was at war allied with Napoleon's France against the British and also resentful of the way the South, especially Virginia, dominated the nation's politics since the election of Thomas Jefferson. Andrew Jackson's victory at the Battle of New Orleans and the Treaty of Ghent eventually ending the war ended such talk of New England secession. But nearly 200 years later, the echoes of those discussions resonate again across the region.

Such talk, however, is not pro-Kerry/anti-Bush "blue staters" and liberals looking to either leave the U.S. or join New England with Canada. New Hampshire's Free State Project and Vermont's Second Vermont Republic are on an entirely different track than sore loser politics.

The Free State Project's origins go back to early 2001 when

Yale political science graduate student Jason P. Sorens and other Libertarian activists debated, through round table discussions in *Liberty* magazine and through correspondence, the future of the Libertarian Party after another disappointing general election showing. Such discourse helped to influence his thinking, along with an article on secession written by distinguished George Mason University economist Walter Williams. The Free State Project was born as way to correct both the defects of the LP and take advantage of what seems to be the future politics of decentralization.

"Third parties don't work on a national scale," Sorens said. "Not just because the system is against them, but the culture is too. If you look around the world, the parties and movements that are new and dynamic are the ones promoting regionalism, local culture, separatism and autonomy." [7]

Thus the FSP hopes to correct the basic mistake of the LP by concentrating its members in one state. The LP likes to brag that it's the biggest non-major party simply because it runs the most candidates across the country. Yet it doesn't realize that designation just means more defeats and less chance of influencing national or even local politics. The LP has few regions across the country where its voters or potential voters live in great strength and while libertarians in ideology run the gamut of social, cultural and economic groups from members of biker gangs to computer programmers to inhabitants of nudist colonies, none of these groups are organized or politically conscious enough to provide support for LP candidates. Even worse, those who publicly call themselves libertarians or are even sympathetic to libertarian ideology, will have nothing to do with LP.

By picking New Hampshire as the place to where it will congregate, the FSP didn't just throw a dart on a map. New Hampshire has a tradition of strong local politics through the town meeting form of government. It has no state income tax and punishes politicians who try to call for one. Cutting government is positively looked upon in the Granite State. New

Hampshire's state House of Representatives is one of the largest electoral bodies in the world and getting elected to it is not an onerous or expensive task. Fusion voting is permitted in the state and which allows its non-major parties an opportunity to influence elections. New Hampshire has even elected Libertarians to public office and LP members there have some pull (the state LP chairman John Babiarz was named to a budget-cutting committee by former governor Craig Benson). Beyond these technical matters, lies a deeper significance to New Hampshire as the FSP's ultimate destination.

"We fit well with New Hampshire because it is as close to a libertarian and classical liberal place as you will find in the United States," Sorens said. "They take a tough line here on taxes and government spending. They're for economic growth and there's a culture of tolerance here on social issues. The biggest bias here is against the nanny state, whether it is seat belt laws or gun control."[8]

Such a state, in the cradle of the American Revolution no less, seems perfect for what the FSP wants to do. But Sorens is well aware of the biases that people have against libertarians that have kept the purist LP far away from any kind of power. He and other FSP leaders saw it first hand when a offshoot group of the FSP called the Free Town Project tried to immigrate *en masse* to Grafton, New Hampshire with 200 members by quickly buying up all available land for sale and then announcing plans to eliminate the town's planning board, pull the town out of the local school district and then have the local police NOT enforce any laws on the books against drugs, prostitution, building code violations or mandatory recycling, presumably doing all this on the same day when they arrived. FSP leaders and members were embarrassed and had to disavow not just what the Free Town Project stood for, but the "We're taking over!" attitude they portrayed and have tried to avoid for their own group. Needless to say it was an attitude that did not endear them to the residents of Grafton, who held a stormy town meeting with officials from both groups in June of 2004.

That's why the FSP wants to reach out to state's rights conservatives and pro-decentralization ("Power to the People!") type liberals to broaden their coalition of support within the state and in recruiting new members. Despite setbacks that included the whole FTP fiasco, the loss of Gov. Benson (who personally recruited the FSP to pick New Hampshire over nine other small states) in the 2004 election and the loss of membership by those disappointed in the selection of New Hampshire, the group was only several hundred short of reaching its goal of 7,000 members by the start of 2005. A big recruiting push scheduled for the same year is the hope the FSP has to send it on its way to its goal of 20,000 members by 2008. The FSP's example has also spawned several imitators, including Christian Exodus, which wants to recruit thousands of Christian conservatives to move to South Carolina to become activists in promoting that state's second secession from the U.S.

"We're well beyond the point of no return," Sorens said. "I think we've got a lot of people committed to moving here regardless if we reach the 20,000 mark that even if we don't make it, we'll still have a pool of activists working throughout the state to reach our goals, whether it's working through their local town meetings or through the New Hampshire Liberty Alliance political group."

So what would the FSP do with their "freedom"? Opium dens on every corner? Privatized police forces? Local schools shut down? Hardly. The FSP is not about forcing so-called libertarian lifestyles on places unwilling to receive them (something the clueless FTP people were unable to figure out). All the FSP wishes to do is to let communities develop and live the way they wish while eliminating wasteful government programs, needless taxes, ending collaboration between state and local officials in enforcing unconstitutional laws such as the Patriot Act, removing federal control over state lands, preventing asset forfeiture and abuses of eminent domain by local government officials and law enforcement agencies, revoke inefficient state regulations and monopolies, asking for state control over immigration and try to negotiate directly with the federal government for more autonomy by opting out of national programs like the No Child Left Behind Act in favor of tax rebates or block grants.

The Free State will also seek to assert itself in foreign policy by not allowing New Hampshire's National Guard units to be used in foreign conflicts that are not declared wars by Congress and reject treaties that undermined New Hampshire's economic, political or cultural interests, especially those that are negotiated through the United Nations. They also wish to negotiate trade agreements with other provinces and states like itself around the globe.

If the FSP is seen as a radical solution to the problems non-major parties have, then it certainly fits into the country's history if you consider the Kentucky and Virginia Resolutions of 1799 to the Alien and Sedition Acts radical, or former Vice-President John C. Calhoun's Fort Hill Address of 1831 radical, or the migration of the Mormons from Nauvoo, Illinois to Utah as radical or other such cultural and political migrations such as New York liberals to Vermont or South Florida, Midwest conservatives along with "Okies" and "Arkies" to California and then back out again to Texas, Idaho and other states in the mountain West, or African-Americans from the rural South to the industrial North as radical too. Indeed, what the Free State Project envisions is what they like to believe the Founding Fathers and subsequently Calhoun (who, like Sorens, graduated from Yale) saw the states as being in the new Union, the breaks on expansive federal power and as what the early Progressives saw the states and local governments as being, laboratories for public policy. In so doing, the FSP is also reconciling the two biggest pulls in U.S. culture, both its rootlessness and its determination to seek out the like-minded and the similar.

"A lot of the rootlessness and restlessness one finds in the American psyche has to do with economic factors, such as finding that good paying job, for example. But there are also cultural factors as well," Sorens said. "People desire that place they can call home, where they can settle with people that have similar cultural backgrounds, interests, tastes, anything they can bond with their neighbors in a community. Or maybe become something they couldn't wherever they used to live. Or just start over in someplace new. That's why I think people search so long for that home that they can love and that's what we're trying to provide in New Hampshire for those who are liberty minded where they can't find any place else."

The FSP does not call for secession from the United Sates nor does it promote it. It is vehicle for decentralization. Yet in the wake of the Bush victory last fall, a few, especially on the left, are calling for secession of their particular states and or regions. The irony is, of course, delicious because such calls for secession would have certainly been rejected by the same people in the wake of a John Kerry victory. Many leftists, until now, have relegated secession and decentralization onto the taboo list and have attacked those who have had the nerve to broach such subjects, as the League of the South can attest to in their running battles with the Southern Poverty Law Center (SPLC).

Such talk of secession is again the knee-jerk reaction of those disappointed in the outcome of the recent presidential election and will ultimately come to nothing. But if there was a place that could potentially secede from the U.S., it is Vermont. Is this because the Green Mountain State voted 60 percent for Kerry? No. It's because from 1777 to 1791, Vermont took its place among the nations of the world.

The Second Vermont Republic, which traces its origins to an anti-war rally at Johnson State College in 2003, does not plan to run candidates in the next election nor become a political action committee. What it does intend to do is to educate the citizens of the state of their unique status of one-time independence in the past and their potential for uniqueness in the future, whether as an independent republic or not.

"We're more of a movement than we are a political party," Thomas Naylor, a former Duke University economist and head of the Second Vermont Republic said. "We're certainly not going to be running candidates any time soon. We're about education. Abraham Lincoln did a number on secession whether it was to wrongly declare it unconstitutional, make it politically unfeasible or to say that a small place like Vermont can't survive economically by itself. We want to change all that thinking. If we can do so, then that will ultimately lead us down the road where the day comes when town meetings across the state vote in favor of resolutions calling for secession from the United States." [9]

This education will include the real Ethan Allen, Vermont nationalist, selfish individualist and American patriot all in one alongside the debate on whether Allen wanted Vermont to join the U.S., be independent or join with Canada. It will also include the fact that Vermont sent delegates to the Hartford Convention and that in 1858 Vermont was one of a dozen states that nullified the Fugitive Slave Act by refusing to allow its public officials to arrest runaway slaves.

"Vermont was made from scratch. We were never a colony," Naylor said. "That's our heritage and we have to promote it. We have a big education job ahead of us and we're barely a year old. What we also hope to see is pro-secession or pro-decentralization efforts spin off from us to more active grassroots political organizations."

If so, then the Second Vermont Republic has already had big impact in a year's time. The group's Middlebury Declaration, its written goals for Vermont independence drafted during a meeting of the group in November of 2004 in the town of Middlebury, has been cited in several foreign publications, particularly in neighboring Quebec. Prominent stories in the leading French opinion magazine *LaDevoir* and the CBC in

Montreal, allowed the group to establish contacts with the Bloc Quebecois and Parti' Québécois pro-secession parties from Quebec. A write-up in *The Nation* has produced interest from around the country and, unsolicited according to Naylor, statements of intent from leftists to move to Vermont. It spun off efforts by grassroots activists to make Vermont's Independence Day, which is Jan. 15, 1775, into a statewide holiday and to put a resolution before the spring 2005 town meetings to call for all Vermont National Guard troops to be removed from Iraq.

But to those who think this is going to be some leftist Eden declaring itself independent, Naylor will happily point out that while Kerry did indeed carry Vermont overwhelmingly, the conservative Republican governor Jim Douglas and lieutenant governor Brian Dubie won re-election, also with 60 percent of the vote. What the Second Vermont Republic comes down to, even if secession doesn't take place, is seeking an answer to the question, what is the best way to preserve this unique place?

"Vermonters see themselves as unique and Vermont as a place shows the world that small is beautiful. One can live happily in a place with small churches, small towns and small businesses," Naylor said. "And yet, the National Register for Historic Places says the whole state is on an endangered list thanks to creeping development. We held off Wal-Mart for a number of years and yet that pressure for development combined with the Interstate Commerce Clause and other statutes make it hard for a state to preserve itself as it wishes to. That's why secession may be the only way out to preserve what we have. But we also have to realize that there are four Wal-Marts here, not just one. There is obviously a demand for them in this state and that's why the education aspect to the Second Vermont Republic is so important to get our residents to realize who and what they are hurting when they shop there."

Primary Colors (The Club for Growth)

Progressives viewed the party primary as a way they could take the power of deciding who gets on the ballot for an election from the bosses and grant it to the rank and file members of that party. Likewise, the members of the Non-Partisan League used the primary process to advance their agenda and their candidates. Discovering the primary as a path to political power (outside of the presidential process) has been groups like the Club for Growth.

One of the new 527 political groups started by pro-supply side economic conservatives and headed by Stephen Moore, an aide to former Congressman Dick Armey and a fellow at both the Cato Institute and the Heritage Foundation, the Club made an impact on the 2004 election cycle by nearly pulling off a huge upset. Incumbent Pennsylvania Senator Arlen Specter needed assistance from President Bush and from his Keystone State colleague Rick Santorum to save himself from defeat from Congressman Pat Toomey in the GOP primary. It was the money provided by the Club that made Toomey's challenge possible. And it was money well spent according to Moore.

"There's no question a primary is a cheaper venue than a general election to make an impact politically," Moore said. "The voting base is going to be more ideological given that many primaries are closed to just party members only. A lot of interest groups and voter groups really don't get involved in them and it's an easier way to reach voting bases you're trying to turn out." [10]

The Club has discovered what the NPL discovered a long time ago, that winning a primary in many cases is tantamount to winning a general election. Electoral districts for state and national offices have now been so gerrymandered to favor one of the major parties or the other, that winning that primary becomes a golden ticket to election in most cases. Having that Republican or Democratic label to run on makes the investment in the primary worth it. A case in point was the Club-backed candidate Tom Colburn. A former Oklahoma Congressman who ran for the U.S Senate in 2004, Colburn made plenty of gaffes on the campaign trail. But because he was successful in routing the GOP establishment candidate (former Oklahoma City Mayor Kirk Humphries) in the primary, his holding of that Republican label was more than enough to carry him to a general election victory as President Bush led the state GOP ticket with over 60 percent of the vote.

"What we want to do is put the candidates we back in a position to win and a position to have influence in the direction of the Republican Party," Moore said. "We target those Republicans who we believe are not following in the pro-growth policies of Ronald Reagan of low taxes and low government spending, or RINOs (Republicans in Name Only) as they are commonly called by conservatives, and try to defeat them in primaries like Specter. Or we try to back candidates in open races where there isn't an incumbent running. We feel we're moving the party in the right direction and putting the fear of God in the RINOs and would-be RINOs out there."

The Club saw its dues paying membership soar from 1,500 to 9,000 during 2004 and it won 15 of 17 targeted races. It will have a big influence over many of the freshman Republican senators and members of the House having backed them for election. Moore feels the Club, along with other 527 groups and those outside the party process, are going to have the biggest influence on the political parties.

"We are the wave of the future," Moore said. "The new campaign laws have helped us and other 527 groups like EMILY's List and Move On.org, while curbing the influence of the parties. Unlike a lot of these groups, we've been more directly involved with the primary process, especially with the Republicans, but we would support any Democrat who held similar views to our own."

And if more such groups like the Club for Growth discover what they've discovered about party primaries, such elections will take on a special importance as a way those outside the two major parties can influence U.S. politics.

The Loyal Opposition (Green and Constitution Parties)
While this author may not be very optimistic of the chances that non-major parties have to be on par or even supplant the majors, two of these parties do have the opportunity to still be players in the U.S. political game. The Greens and the Constitution Party have ideological and cultural bases, or at least the potential of having such bases, along with the regional support that allows them to have an impact. All the remaining non-major parties, Libertarians included, simply don't have such voting blocs and unless they develop them, remain doomed to irrelevance.

Green Party activist Ben Manski represents the crossroads the Green Party faced in 2004 and the path they intend to take in 2005 and beyond. Manski had been a big supporter of Ralph Nader when he was the Green Party nominee in 1996 and 2000. Yet in 2004, Nader at first decided to eschew the Greens to run as a pure independent. Realizing the difficulty of doing this, along with picking up the endorsement of the remnants of the Reform Party, Nader reconsidered his stance and tried to at least get the Greens' endorsement for President. But the Greens would have nothing to do with Nader this time. At their summer convention in Manski's home state of Wisconsin, Manski and his fellow Greens rejected Nader's bid on the floor of the Midwest Airlines Center in Milwaukee and went for an unknown California lawyer named David Cobb instead.

Cobb's dismal performance at the polls along with the split with Nader-backers may seem like bad omens for Greens, but Manski isn't seeing them. Instead he's turning his attention to 2005, and 2007 and 2009. These, you will note, are off-year elections or when local elections usually take place and it is here that the Greens are at their most powerful. By winning such elections to school boards, city councils or county commissions, the Greens have been able to affect policy at the local level that can have an impact on national politics. The whole homosexual marriage debate in many ways was pushed to the forefront by the Greens thanks to a Green mayor of New Paltz, New York and to the strong challenge by Green candidate Matt Gonzales for the mayoralty of San Francisco ultimately won by Democrat Gavin Newsome, who was allowing such marriages in city hall. The anti-smoking ordinances for local bars and restaurants have the color Green on them (One of the cities where one such anti-smoking ordinance was enacted was in Duluth, Minn. where *Minneapolis Star-Tribune* political writer Dane Smith commented "The Greens practically run the Duluth City Council.")

That the Greens have been so successful in enacting their agenda in this way shows that they are the strongest of the non-major parties. They have done this by identifying voting blocs and mobilizing them to the polls. Such blocs include leftists, alternative lifestyle seekers (non-conformists to their friends, weirdos to everyone else) well-educated, upper-middle class whites in college towns and mid-sized cities, plus members of public employee's unions in such places.

"It's true that we have a cohesive world view and have set ourselves up as an alternative party for those on the left," Manski said. "But we've been successful in moderate sized cities that have a tradition of public involvement in politics and have a large group of public employees. We've been able to establish multi-racial coalitions in those places. We've been able to elect candidates in small and medium sized towns and we've shown strength in rural areas as well. In Wisconsin for example, there are a high percentage of Greens in places like La Crosse, the Kickapoo River Valley and in Polk County." [11]

La Crosse, the Kickapoo River Valley and Polk County. If that sounds like the same well-worn path Wisconsin Progressives once traveled on in the western part of the state during a campaign you are correct. Manski knows it's no coincidence that the Greens are doing well in places where the Progressives were once strong. He sees the Greens as being their descendents, along with being the immediate descendents of other leftist groups in the state like the Wisconsin Alliance and the Farm-Labor Party. In being part of this family, the Greens have done their best in the progressive strongholds of Madison and Dane County where, taking advantage of the non-partisan status of local elections, (a reform enacted by the early progressives) they have been able to work with leftist Democrats in a coalition known as Progressive Dane. Formed in the late 1990s, Progressive Dane blunted a seeming conservative trend coming from Madison's outlying exurbs by electing candidates to the county board (Manski was nearly elected to the county board in 1996) along with candidates to local village boards and city councils. Green activists helped elect current Madison Mayor Dave Cieslewicz and made possible the unilateral rise in Madison's minimum wage to $7.25 per hour, which is $2.10 higher than it is nationally. (Dane County's Democratic Party leadership however, wants to end the party's cooperation with the Greens in local elections. They were incensed that the Greens ran candidates against theirs in recent elections for county offices.)

"There's no question the Greens come out of the new social movements of the 1970s whether its feminism, environmentalism and new labor organizations. It comes out of that tradition," Manski said. "I think organizing the Green Party in a place like the Upper Midwest is easier than in most places because you have the tradition of independent political parties like the Progressives and the Farm-Labor Party, it's easier to get on the ballot up here and you have non-partisan elections here. The Greens fit into that same zeitgeist. It's part of our identity."

And preserving that identity is why Manski is not interested in seeing the Greens trying to influence Democratic Party politics outside the realm of something like Progressive Dane, local alliances for non-partisan races. Like it or not, for county, state and national offices, the Dems will have to accept the fact the Greens will be their competitors on the left and will have to deal with them.

"Ballot access laws in many states forces you to run someone for president just to stay on," Manski said. "And I am of the opinion that a presidential campaign, even a losing a one, is a great way to promote your party to people all over the country. Look at what Nader's two runs for the White House on the Green Party ticket have done to expand our membership. And that's why I don't feel that having Green activists working for either Howard Dean or Dennis Kucinich would have made any difference either way and is not a good use of our time and resources. The Democrats simply will not nominate a true progressive to head their party. You saw what they did to Dean. The last such progressive to lead the party, George McGovern, the party leadership sabotaged him from the moment he won the nomination. The Democrats are just as responsible for the war in the Iraq and for the Patriot Act as the Republicans are. I'm not interested in what they're doing. We're going to try and expand from beyond our citadels to be an influential political party.

"Now, if there are Democrats who we feel are very progressive or share most of our views and positions on issues, then obviously we're not going stretch our limited resources running against them, like a Russ Feingold for example (Manski feels the Minnesota Green Party made a mistake running a candidate against Paul Wellstone in 2002) and you can take that as an endorsement. We're also not interested in fusion politics either. The Greens in New York don't run fusion tickets with other parties because the third parties there use it as a king-making process that tries to get spoils for themselves in return for their support. That's power bloc politics and that's not what we're about."

What the Greens are about, according to Manski, is participatory, grassroots democracy and their strong position in local government in the areas where they are strongest in numbers puts them in a position to benefit from the new politics of decentralization and states rights the left has suddenly "discovered" in the wake of the Bush victory. One particular bottom-up change can that help the party expand their influence to more races is instant run-off voting.

"It's an election reform we are pushing strongly," Manski said. "In instant run-off voting, you have choice preferences so you can make a meaningful vote for a third party candidate as well as vote for the major party candidate you think will probably win as well, so there's no such thing as a 'wasted' vote. I think it would be a real benefit to democracy. We hope as more and more communities adopt it for their elections, it will become a wide-spread practice that will force itself up to the state and national level."

The Greens are more of a movement than they are an organized political party. As Manski points out they have chapters in over a 100 countries around the world and thus its members will think more in idealistic terms than in calculated political decisions designed to win elections or gain power to preserve the movement character and keep it safe from co-optation (although a majority of German Greens forgot their pacifism when it came to supporting the use of the *Luftwaffe* to bomb Serbia in 1999 just as Hitler had done during the World War II in order to be a part the ruling coalition, a calculated political decision that shows the sometimes corrupting effects of power on human beings regardless of their beliefs).

The Constitution Party, on the other hand, is a political party in search of a movement. Born out of the splits in the Republican Party and the conservative moment in the late 1980s and early 1990s, (its first and only presidential candidate up to 2004 was former Nixon Administration official and Moral Majority founder Howard Phillips) the CP was created to revive interest in conservative third-party politics after it gone moribund in the 1980s as Ronald Reagan incorporated such elements into his winning coalition and after party's like the Populist (which ran David Duke for President in 1988), the American Independent and the American Party descended into extremism. Twelve years after its founding it has become the largest and most conservative legitimate alternative to the Republican Party as the Greens have become to the Democrats. Now it just has to convince the majority of conservative voters and activists of that fact.

"The Christian Coalition wouldn't even list our presidential candidate, Michael Peroutka, in their voter's guides," CP

National Chairman James Clymer said. "And when I ran for the U.S. Senate in Pennsylvania in 2004, I was the only pro-life candidate in the field and I couldn't even get an endorsement from the Pennsylvania Pro-Life League."[12]

Despite being snubbed a pro-life group, Clymer was still able to win more than 200,000 votes and nearly tipped the election away from incumbent Arlen Specter. Unlike the Greens, the CP showed flexibility in trying to influence a major party primary by endorsing Specter's GOP primary opponent Pat Toomey. Yet, such a Rodney Dangerfield-like existence of no-respect from the media, the majors and even the voters, is common for anyone, candidate, party leader or activist, of a non-major party. But that may change in future. That's because in many electoral districts, such non-major parties like the Greens and the CP (and the LP if they ever rediscover their opposition to big government and leave the lifestyle questions to the Greens and their constituency.) are going to be the only opposition available to the major parties. Gerrymandering of districts has helped to create this situation where there are only a few competitive state legislative or Congressional seats for both the major parties to fight over. That plus the slow collapse and decrepitude of some major party structures in places like Texas for the Democrats and Illinois for the Republicans for example, give non-major parties opportunities to rise above their non-major status, if not at least to preserve some semblance of democracy in such places.

"The GOP is out of excuses," Clymer said. "They control the national government and if, over the next four years, things don't get better in the country from a social standpoint than they are now, if Roe vs. Wade is not overturned or if gay marriage is still a big issue or is in place in certain localities, then I think many conservatives are going to say 'Hey, wait a minute!' and that will be our opportunity to make our pitch. Especially among younger conservatives who are not so set in their ways like the older ones are that they might be influenced to vote for us instead of the GOP."

Such younger conservatives can be found among homeschoolers, which is a growing subgroup that CP wants to penetrate along with groups like Orthodox Christians, industrial labor unions and businesses hurt by free trade policies and those groups determined to preserve Second Amendments rights. Clymer acknowledges the CP's failure to make deep inroads in such groups so far, along with the broader conservative voting bloc. The polarization of two major parties on cultural and class issues makes such efforts difficult for any non-major party to make their appeals as fear and hatred of the other side often keeps such voters in-line and away from "wasting their vote." But another problem is that of credibility, especially when ideological non-major parties, left and right, tend to splinter apart. Sometimes such fissures are on serious philosophical questions and other times they are trivial, mostly personality clashes. The CP tried to rectify that situation on the right by engaging in a unification process with other non-major parties like the America First Party, the American Party and the Independent American Party. The CCCC or Clarion Call to Convergence Committee, had meetings in the fall of 2004 to begin the legally difficult process of bringing such parties together, if not getting them to work more closely. It hasn't worked out.

"It easy to see why such parties split because it takes a special kind of person to break out of the two-party mode," Clymer said. "They have to be opinionated, ideological, principled and willing to be a maverick. Well, try to have all these same kinds of people in the same party together and you can see why it's difficult to keep them from splitting apart. Those of us in the third party movement have to be strong enough to put up with each other's differences like the major parties do or we're never going to get anywhere."

Conclusion—The New Politics

The major story in the aftermath of the 2004 election, ideologically at least, was the reclassification on the left of "state's rights" and "decentralization" from their forbidden realm back into the real world. In this way, such terms now have a legitimacy that they didn't have when they were in the exclusive realm of the right. This transformation has occurred just as the "governing" right, or the coalition of neoconservatives, conservative Christians and Republican functionaries, has gradually abandoned such politics ever since the failed federal government shutdown during the budget negotiations of 1995 and have increased their hold on central power since the 2004 election. The end result will be a new politics emerging based both on the traditional—trying to shift power from the central government to state and local governments—and on the new—trying affect political changes from the bottom up (in essence, the Green Party strategy.) In this new politics, non-major parties and political movements aforementioned in the previous chapter are well positioned to benefit. Thus, the new struggles really won't be between traditional left-right poles, but between centralists and decentralists.

What this book has shown through its look at successful non-major political parties of the past such as the Non-Partisan League of North Dakota, the Farm-Labor Party of Minnesota and the Progressives of Wisconsin, is that the success of these parties was largely due to their regional and local character. And it is no accident as to why. These parties were able win the support of local cultural and economic voting blocs that made up key sectors of the electorate in their respective states. They were also able to benefit from the lack of a strong major party alternative within their respective states. Such conditions are presenting themselves again today and conditions are ripe for a revival of such parties, or for the growth in strength of other non-major political parties and their abilities to influence the majors, which is has been their traditional and still today role in U.S. politics.

Even if you don't want to look back to the early part of the 20th century and to the states of North Dakota, Wisconsin and Minnesota, there are plenty of other examples to choose from.

The State's Rights Party of 1948 and George Wallace's American Independent Party both were Southern regional movements that had a profound effect on the future of politics in that region. It facilitated the decline of the Democratic Party in the South and led to the rise of the Republicans. Wallace's American Independent Party (AIP) and subsequent campaigns for the Democratic Party's presidential nomination expanded upon that Southern base by reaching into economic and cultural groups such as white ethnics, Catholics, industrial, trade and craft union workers in the urban centers of the North.

Two independent political parties of New York, Liberal and Conservative, took advantage of that state's fusion ballot and elected candidates in the 1960s and 70s such Liberal John Lindsey as Mayor of New York City and Conservative James L. Buckley as U.S. Senator.

The Progressive Coalition in Vermont has been successful in re-electing Bernie Sanders to the U.S. House of Representatives since 1990 and has also elected members to the Vermont state legislature. Sanders, like many Vermont liberals an ex-pat from New York, built that coalition through his terms as mayor of the state's largest city, Burlington, and it's active in local politics throughout the state.

In 1990 two other state-wide political movements also elected governors. Former Secretary of the Interior Walter Hickel won the governorship of Alaska on the Alaskan Independence Party ticket and Former U.S. Senator Lowell Weicker became governor of Connecticut leading the ticket of the A Connecticut Party. Then in 1998 came perhaps the crowning achievement of the non-major party movement in the late 20th Century, the election of Jesse Ventura as governor of Minnesota.

Of course what a lot of these examples have common is that like the tornadoes that often describe non-major party activity, their moments of destruction and mayhem of the established political order came and went quickly and the powers that be quickly rebuilt and restored politics as usual. Hickel had no interest in making Alaska an independent state as called for in the AIP platform and simply used the party as vehicle for a political comeback when his own GOP standard was unavailable. That, plus the mysterious disappearance and death of the AIP's founder Joe Vogler, ended the party's effectiveness. The A Connecticut Party could have been a way to unite rich, country-club moderate Republicans and upper-middle class Democrats, but Weicker flip-flopped on a state income tax issue. That, plus a castor oil and gruel state budget in 1991 that may have saved the state from economic ruin but also drove away anyone who would have stood by Weicker and his party, caused the A Connecticut Party to fade away when Weicker didn't run for re-election in 1994. Ventura was elected on the Reform Party ticket (though the straight-arrow Ross Perot wanted nothing to do with the feather-boa wearing Ventura and gave him no support during the 1998 campaign.) but the subsequent fiasco of the party's presidential nominating process in 2000 drove

Ventura and Minnesota Reform Party Chairman Dean Barkley to form their own party, the Minnesota Independence Party. The IP could have been a vehicle for the kind of suburban and exurban populist issues of taxes, traffic congestion, education, open government and the environment (issues that gubernatorial candidate, Minnesota Attorney General Mike Hatch and the "new" DFL could run on in 2006) that helped elect Ventura in the first place. However, Jesse was more interested in refereeing professional wrestling matches and broadcasting football games in the now-defunct XFL than building a party. When he left the governor's office in 2003, the party shrunk accordingly. As Ben Manski said, the New York state Liberal and Conservative parties are more into spoils and king-making than having the impact they did nearly 40 years ago. Only the Dixiecrat/AIP parties along with the independent political parties of the Upper Midwest have had political impacts that have lasted to this day.

Nevertheless, the success of such regional and cultural based politics is the most proven way that non-major political parties and movements can make their impact felt in U.S. politics. Indeed, the new politics may become a welcome respite for those who will weary of the stalemated "culture wars" by 2008. After the 2004 campaign, it's become increasingly clear that many Americans hate their fellow Americans more so than they do Osama bin Laden, who murdered 3,000 of their own countrymen. Not even that awful morning on Sept. 11, 2001, was able to unite the country for very long as the old divisions that go back for a long time (as the Swift Boat Veterans controversy proved) reared their ugly heads once again.

And yet, in this age of cellular phones, fax machines, emails, the internet and other instant communications designed to shrink the world around us, we forget how large the country we inhabit together really is. The author was reminded of this fact traveling the long distances through the hill country of southeast and south-central North Dakota conducting interviews for this book. If we are such a big country, why do so many have the "This town isn't big enough for the both us!" attitude? Why do so many politicians and activists have the "BE LIKE US OR ELSE!" mentality?

If there is something like a paleoconservative (or even paleolibertarian) slogan, it was uttered by author and *Chronicles* at-large editor Bill Kauffman "Let Utah be Utah and let San Francisco be San Francisco!" So much of the nation's internal conflicts could be solved in an instant if we followed such advice. It is also the nutshell of the new politics, creating places and spaces in this big country of ours we can carve out our own identities, lasting and real cultures and communities and the politics that go along with them. The centralization of the New Deal ended the independent political parties of the Upper Midwest. But it also spawned the counterrevolution that came with the conservative movement and all that spun off from it cumulating in Ronald Reagan's election in 1980. That political struggle is as dead Reagan is. A new political struggle is being formed after the new proponents of centralism (many of whom are the ideological and cultural inheritors of the New Deal) won the election of 2004. Exploiting the war that began on 9-11, (no matter if undeclared by Congress) they have amassed more power for themselves in Washington that at any time since the Great Society and the Vietnam War. Those who dissent from this power grab, regardless of ideology, region, party, religion or other creed, will make up the other side in this debate. The stakes are nothing less than a United States that reflects what its Founding Father's intended or what new power elite wish it to be.

The independent political parties of the Upper Midwest give us today plenty of clues on being a successful political movement or a non-major party in a two major party system. Unless such non-major parties of today and the future want to remain a mystery, they had better follow them.

Bibliography

CHAPTER 1

1. "Miserable, Sad Day on the Range" by Bill Hanna, Mesabi Daily News, Oct. 25, 2003 online edition. Updated Oct. 25, 2003 at 3:03.55 P.M.
2. All details of the Sen. Wellstone plane crash came from the St. Paul Pioneer Press, Oct. 26, 2002, Vol. 154, No. 184, A Section, p.1A-16A, articles: "Minnesota's Idealist Dies," by Bill Gardner, Philip Pina and Jim Ragsdale; "Experts Suspect Weather and Landing Site Caused Crash," by Tom Majeski
3. Ibid p. 1A-16A, along with article "Tragedy may Shake State and National Power Balance," by Patrick Sweeney on p. 1A
4. Professor Wellstone Goes to Washington by Dennis McGrath and Dane Smith, 1995, University of Minnesota Press, p.17
5. Ibid pp. 2-3
6. Ibid p. xvii
7. Ibid p. 4
8. Ibid p. 5
9. Ibid p. 5
10. Ibid pp. 6-7
11. Ibid pp. 6-7
12. Ibid. p. 30
13. Ibid p. 22
14. Ibid p. 28
15. Ibid pp. 3-4
16. Ibid p. 36
17. Ibid p. 32
18. Ibid pp. 1-3
19. The Almanac of American Politics 1988 by Michael Barone and Grant Ujifusa, National Journal, 1987, p. 625

20. Professor Wellstone Goes to Washington by Dennis McGrath and Dane Smith, 1995, University of Minnesota Press, p.36
21. Ibid p. 18
22. Ibid pp. 19-20
23. Interview with Hy Berman, June 22, 2004, at home in Minneapolis
24. Professor Wellstone Goes to Washington by Dennis McGrath and Dane Smith, 1995, University of Minnesota Press, pp. 19-20
25. Ibid pp. 18-19
26. Interview with Lisa Pattni, July 21, 2004
27. "Miserable, Sad Day on the Range" by Bill Hanna, Mesabi Daily News, Oct. 25, 2003 online edition. Updated Oct. 25, 2003 at 3:03.55 P.M.
28. Interview with Lisa Pattni, July 21, 2004, over-the-phone
29. Interview with Dane Smith, June 22, 2004, at Minnesota State Capitol in St. Paul
30. Ibid
31. Ibid
32. The LaFollettes of Wisconsin - Love and Politics in Progressive America by Bernard A. Weisberger, 1994, University of Wisconsin Press p. 3
33. Ibid p. 59
34. The Political Career of Floyd B. Olson by George H. Mayer, Minnesota State Historical Society Press, St. Paul, 1951, p. xii
35. Ibid p. xii
36. Ibid p. Xiv
37. Interview with Bill Kretschmar, June 30, 2004, Ashley, North Dakota
38. Professor Wellstone Goes to Washington by Dennis McGrath and Dane Smith, 1995, University of Minnesota Press, p. xv
39. Ibid p. xix
40. Ibid p. xiv

41. ibid p.m. xiv
42. The Almanac of American Politics 1988 by Michael Barone and Grant Ujifusa, National Journal, 1987, p. 626
43. Professor Wellstone Goes to Washington by Dennis McGrath and Dane Smith, 1995, University of Minnesota Press, p. 28
44. Ibid p. xvii
45. Ibid p. xxii
46. Ibid p. 253-258
47. Interview with Dane Smith, June 22, 2004, Minnesota State Capitol in St. Paul

CHAPTER 2

1. *America in Search of Itself* - The Making of the Presidency 1956-1980 by Theodore H. White, 1982, Harper and Row, pp.169-171
2. Politics at the Periphery - Third Parties in Two-Party America by J. David Gillespie, University of South Carolina Press, 1993 p. 243
3. The Making of the President 1968 by Theodore H. White, 1969, Atheneum p. 63
4. America in Search of Itself - The Making of the Presidency 1956-1980 by Theodore H. White, 1982, Harper and Row, p. 49
5. Politics at the Periphery - Third Parties in Two-Party America by J. David Gillespie, University of South Carolina Press, 1993 p. 193
6. Presidential Campaigns by Paul F. Boller, Oxford University Press, 1984, p. 13
7. Main-Traveled Roads by Hamlin Garland, Harper and Row, 1922, pp. 54-56
8. Wisconsin's Past and Present - A Historical Atlas - The Wisconsin Cartographers Guild, The University of Wisconsin Press, 1998 p. 43, pp. 72-73
9. Politics in Wisconsin by Leon Epstein, University of Wisconsin Press, 1958, p. 2

10. Wisconsin's Past and Present - A Historical Atlas - The Wisconsin Cartographers Guild, The University of Wisconsin Press, 1998 pp. 72-73

11. Cooperative Commonwealth - Co-ops in Rural Minnesota 1859-1939 by Steve Kellior, Minnesota Historical Society Press, 2000, p. 6

12. Ibid pp. 6-8

13. Ibid p. 7

14. Ibid p. 14

15. Ibid pp. 310-311

16. *The Cousins' Wars* - Religion, Politics, and the Triumph of Anglo-America by Kevin Phillips, Basic Books, 1999 p. 399

17. They Chose Minnesota - A Survey of the State's Ethnic Groups by June Drenning Holmquist, Minnesota State Historical Society Press, 1981, p.309

18. The German-American Heritage by Irene Franck and David Brownstone. Facts on File, 1989 pp. 29-30

19. *The Cousins' Wars* - Religion, Politics, and the Triumph of Anglo-America by Kevin Phillips, Basic Books, 1999 pp. 553-559

20. The German-American Heritage by Irene Franck and David Brownstone. Facts on File, 1989 pp. 29-30

21 From Norway to America - A History of the Migration by Ingrid Semmingsen, Translated from Norwegian by Eina Haugen, University of Minnesota Press, 1978 pp. 121-122

22. Ibid pp.34-35

23. Ibid p. 8

24. The German-American Heritage by Irene Franck and David Brownstone. Facts on File, 1989 pp. 27-29

25. Ibid pp. 101-103

26. Interview with Hy Berman, June 22, 2004, at home in Minneapolis

27. *The Cousins' Wars* - Religion, Politics, and the Triumph of Anglo-America by Kevin Phillips, Basic Books, 1999 pp. 91-100

28. Wisconsin's Past and Present - A Historical Atlas - The Wisconsin Cartographers Guild, The University of Wisconsin

Press, 1998 pp. 18-19, pp. 30-31

29. They Chose Minnesota - A Survey of the State's Ethnic Groups by June Drenning Holmquist, Minnesota State Historical Society Press, 1981, pp. 163-168

30. *The Cousins' Wars* - Religion, Politics, and the Triumph of Anglo-America by Kevin Phillips, Basic Books, 1999 p. 411

31. The Populist Persuasion by Michael Kazin, Basic Books, 1995, pp. 111-112

32. Ibid pp. 116-117

33. The Political Career of Floyd B. Olson by George H. Mayer, Minnesota State Historical Society Press, St. Paul, 1951, p. 8

34. The German-American Heritage by Irene Franck and David Brownstone. Facts on File, 1989 pp. 107-110

35. *The Cousins' Wars* - Religion, Politics, and the Triumph of Anglo-America by Kevin Phillips, Basic Books, 1999 pp. 549-550

36. Ibid p. 548

37. From Norway to America - A History of the Migration by Ingrid Semmingsen, Translated from Norwegian by Eina Haugen, University of Minnesota Press, 1978 p. 96

38. *The Cousins' Wars* - Religion, Politics, and the Triumph of Anglo-America by Kevin Phillips, Basic Books, 1999 p. 435

39. Ibid pp. 551-559

40. Wisconsin's Past and Present - A Historical Atlas - The Wisconsin Cartographers Guild, The University of Wisconsin Press, 1998 p. 19

CHAPTER 3

1. "The Other Germans Once Filled North Dakota" by Karen Herzog Bismarck Tribune Dec. 26, 1997. Online edition.

2. Minnesota's Farm-Laborism - The Third Party Alternative by Millard Gieske, University of Minnesota Press, 1979, p. 11

3. "Non-Partisanship," By Sean Scallon, *Chronicles: A Magazine of American Culture*, Feb. 2002, Vol. 26, No. 2, pp. 43-44 (This article is the genesis for Beating the Powers that Be. Information

came from interviews from David Danbom, Professor of Political Science at North Dakota State University and Lloyd Ohmdahl, former Lieutenant Governor, Tax Commissioner and political science professor at the University of North Dakota. All quotations from Danbom and Ohmdahl came from interviews conducted in September of 2001).

4. Ibid p. 43

5. Politics at the Periphery - Third Parties in Two-Party America by J. David Gillespie, University of South Carolina Press, 1993 p. 242

6. *The Cousins' Wars* - Religion, Politics, and the Triumph of Anglo-America by Kevin Phillips, Basic Books, 1999 p. 554

7. "Non-Partisanship," By Sean Scallon, *Chronicles: A Magazine of American Culture*, Feb. 2002, Vol. 26, No. 2, pp. 43-44

8. The Populist Persuasion by Michael Kazin, Basic Books, 1995, p. 68

9. "Non-Partisanship," By Sean Scallon, *Chronicles: A Magazine of American Culture*, Feb. 2002, Vol. 26, No. 2, pp. 43-44

10. The North Dakota Political Tradition by Thomas Howard, Editor, Iowa State University Press, 1981 p. 88

11. Ibid pp. 91-92

12. Never Stop Running - Allard K. Lowenstein and the Struggle to Save American Liberalism by William Chafe, Basic Books, 1993, p. 387

13. The North Dakota Political Tradition by Thomas Howard, Editor, Iowa State University Press, 1981 p. 127

14. "The Other Germans Once Filled North Dakota" by Karen Herzog Bismarck Tribune Dec. 26, 1997. Online edition.

15. Non-Partisanship," By Sean Scallon, *Chronicles: A Magazine of American Culture*, Feb. 2002, Vol. 26, No. 2, pp. 43-44

16. "The Other Germans Once Filled North Dakota" by Karen Herzog Bismarck Tribune Dec. 26, 1997. Online edition.

17. Interview with Bill Kretschmar. All comments and information from him in this chapter come in an interview that took place on June 30, 2004 in Ashley, North Dakota

18. The North Dakota Political Tradition by Thomas Howard, Editor, Iowa State University Press, 1981 p. 132
19. Ibid pp. 127 and 129
20. "The Other Germans Once Filled North Dakota" by Karen Herzog Bismarck Tribune Dec. 26, 1997. Online edition.
21. The North Dakota Political Tradition by Thomas Howard, Editor, Iowa State University Press, 1981 pp.136-137
22. The *Inter-County Leader*, Vol. 2, May 3, 1934, p. 2
23. Presidential Campaigns by Paul F. Boller, Oxford University Press, 1984, p. 241-242
24. The Populist Persuasion by Michael Kazin, Basic Books, 1995, p. 124
25. The Political Career of Floyd B. Olson by George H. Mayer, Minnesota State Historical Society Press, St. Paul, 1951, p. xviii
26. The LaFollettes of Wisconsin - Love and Politics in Progressive America by Bernard A. Weisberger, 1994, University of Wisconsin Press p. 242
27. Presidential Campaigns by Paul F. Boller, Oxford University Press, 1984, p. 220
28. Politics at the Periphery - Third Parties in Two-Party America by J. David Gillespie, University of South Carolina Press, 1993 pp. 88-89
29. Ibid p. 88
30. Ibid p. 89
31. Ibid p. 89
32. Presidential Campaigns by Paul F. Boller, Oxford University Press, 1984, pp. 241-242 and the The Populist Persuasion by Michael Kazin, Basic Books, 1995, p. 125
33. The North Dakota Political Tradition by Thomas Howard, Editor, Iowa State University Press, 1981 pp.135-137
34. Ibid pp. 137, 141-144
35. "Non-Partisanship," By Sean Scallon, *Chronicles: A Magazine of American Culture*, Feb. 2002, Vol. 26, No. 2, pp. 43-44

CHAPTER 4

1. They Chose Minnesota - A Survey of the State's Ethnic Groups by June Drenning Holmquist, Minnesota State Historical Society Press, 1981, pp. 164 and 227
2. Interview with Hy Berman, June 22, 2004 in Minneapolis
3. Politics at the Periphery - Third Parties in Two-Party America by J. David Gillespie, University of South Carolina Press, 1993 p. 136
4. Interview with Dane Smith, June 22, 2004, State Capitol Building in St. Paul
5. Milwaukee 150 - The Greater Milwaukee Story by Ellen Langhill and Dave Jensen, Milwaukee Publishing Group, 1996, pp. 49-53
6. Before the Storm - Barry Goldwater and the Unmaking of the American Consensus by Rick Perlstein, Hill and Wang, 2001, pp. 34-36
7. Wisconsin's Past and Present - A Historical Atlas - The Wisconsin Cartographers Guild, The University of Wisconsin Press, 1998, pp. 20-21
8. Minnesota's Farm-Laborism - The Third Party Alternative by Millard Gieske, University of Minnesota Press, 1979, p. 20
9. Ibid, p. 13
10. Ibid, p. 7
11. Lindbergh of Minnesota - A Political Biography 1907-1918 by Bruce Larsen, Harcourt, Brace and Jovanovich, 1973 p. 247
12. Ibid, p. 224
13. Ibid p. 235
14. Minnesota's Farm-Laborism - The Third Party Alternative by Millard Gieske, University of Minnesota Press, 1979, pp. 45-46 and The Political Career of Floyd B. Olson by George H. Mayer, Minnesota State Historical Society Press, St. Paul, 1951, pp. 23-24   15. Ibid, p. 15
16. Ibid, pp. 28-30
17. Ibid, pp. 31-32

18. Ibid, pp. 33 and 35
19. Ibid, p. 37
20. Ibid, pp. 40-42
21. Ibid, p. 38
22. Ibid, p. 38
23. Ibid, p. 160
24. Politics at the Periphery - Third Parties in Two-Party America by J. David Gillespie, University of South Carolina Press, 1993 pp. 247-250
25. Ibid, p. 249
26. The Political Career of Floyd B. Olson by George H. Mayer, Minnesota State Historical Society Press, St. Paul, 1951, p. 238
27. Politics at the Periphery - Third Parties in Two-Party America by J. David Gillespie, University of South Carolina Press, 1993 pp. 247
28. The Political Career of Floyd B. Olson by George H. Mayer, Minnesota State Historical Society Press, St. Paul, 1951, p. 239-240
29. Ibid, pp. 242-244
30. Ibid, pp. 278-280
31. Ibid p. xix
32. Politics at the Periphery - Third Parties in Two-Party America by J. David Gillespie, University of South Carolina Press, 1993 pp. 247
33. Ibid p. 251
34. Interview with Hy Berman, June 22, 2004 in Minneapolis
35. Politics at the Periphery - Third Parties in Two-Party America by J. David Gillespie, University of South Carolina Press, 1993 pp. 251
36. Ibid, p. 252
37. Pamphlet written by Hy Berman entitled "Political Anti-Semitism in Minnesota During the Great Depression," Jewish Social Studies, Vol. xxxviii, Summer-Fall, 1976, No. 304
38. Politics at the Periphery - Third Parties in Two-Party America by J. David Gillespie, University of South Carolina Press, 1993 pp. 252

39. Ibid, p. 247
40. Minnesota's Farm-Laborism - The Third Party Alternative by Millard Gieske, University of Minnesota Press, 1979, p. 262
41. Ibid, p. 278
42. Ibid, p. 283
43. Ibid, p. 272
44. "Tired of the Two Parties? Blame Centralization of the Federal Government, not the Constitution" by Pradeep Chhibber and Ken Kollman, Washington Post, Tuesday, Aug. 17, 2004, p. A15
45. The Almanac of American Politics 1988 by Michael Barone and Grant Ujifusa, National Journal, 1987, p. 903
46. Politics in Wisconsin by Leon D. Epstein, University of Wisconsin Press, 1958, p. 51
47. Interview with Margie Hallquist, June 29, 2004, rural Polk County, Wisconsin
48. The Making of the President 1968, by Theodore H. White, Atheneum Publishing, 1969, p. 303
49. Politics in Wisconsin by Leon D. Epstein, University of Wisconsin Press, pp. 80-81
50. America in Search of Itself - The Making of the Presidency 1956-1980 by Theodore H. White, 1982, Harper and Row, p. 51
51. Politics in Wisconsin, by Leon D. Epstein, University of Wisconsin Press, 1958, p. 51
52. The Political Career of Floyd B. Olson by George H. Mayer, Minnesota State Historical Society Press, St. Paul, 1951, pp. 97-98
53. Ibid, p. 111
54. Inside the Wigwam - Chicago Presidential Conventions 1860-1996 by R. Craig Sautter and Edward Burke, Wild Onion Books, 1996, p. 170
55. Interview with Hy Berman, June 22, 2004, Minneapolis
56. Minnesota's Farm-Laborism - The Third Party Alternative by Millard Gieske, University of Minnesota Press, 1979, p. 283
57. Ibid p. 301

58. Ibid p. 287
59. Ibid pp. 324-332
60. Pledging Allegiance - The Last Campaign of the Cold War by Sidney Blumenthal, Harper Perennial, 1991 pp. 112-113.
61. The Almanac of American Politics 1988 by Michael Barone and Grant Ujifusa, National Journal, 1987, pp. 623-624
62. Interview with Hy Berman, June 22, 2004, Minneapolis
63. The Making of the President 1968, by Theodore H. White, Atheneum Publishing, 1969, pp. 76-77, 79
64. Interview with Dane Smith, June 22, 2004, State Capitol Building, St. Paul
65. Ibid

CHAPTER 5

1. Motto - University of Wisconsin-Madison
2. The LaFollettes of Wisconsin - Love and Politics in Progressive America by Bernard A. Weisberger, 1994, University of Wisconsin Press p. xii
3. Wisconsin's Past and Present - A Historical Atlas - The Wisconsin Cartographers Guild, The University of Wisconsin Press, 1998 pp. 72-73
4. The LaFollettes of Wisconsin - Love and Politics in Progressive America by Bernard A. Weisberger, 1994, University of Wisconsin Press pp. 60-61
5. Wisconsin's Past and Present - A Historical Atlas - The Wisconsin Cartographers Guild, The University of Wisconsin Press, 1998, p. 72
6. The *Inter-County Leader* Nov. 2, 1933, Vol. 1, No. 1
7. Interviews with Marge and JoAnn Hallquist, June 26, 2004, Polk County, Wisconsin.
8. The *Inter-County Leader*, Nov. 2, 1933, Vol. 1, No. 1
9. The *Inter-County Leader*, Nov. 9, 1933, Vol. 1, No. 2
10. The *Inter-County Leader*, Nov. 23, 1933, Vol. 1, No. 4
11. The *Inter-County Leader*, May 10, 1934, Vol. 2, No. 19

12. Interview with Robert Dueholm, June 18, 2004 at the offices of the *Inter-County Leader* in Frederic, Wisconsin
13. Wisconsin's Past and Present - A Historical Atlas - The Wisconsin Cartographers Guild, The University of Wisconsin Press, 1998, p. 20
14. Interview with Marge and JoAnn Hallquist, June 26, 2004, Polk County, Wisconsin
15. Interview with Robert Dueholm, June 18, 2004 at the offices of the *Inter-County Leader* in Frederic, Wisconsin
16. Ibid
17. The LaFollettes of Wisconsin - Love and Politics in Progressive America by Bernard A. Weisberger, 1994, University of Wisconsin Press pp. 27-28
18. Ibid pp. 28-29
19. Ibid p. 13
20. Ibid pp. 33-34
21. Milwaukee 150 - The Greater Milwaukee Story by Ellen Langhill and Dave Jensen, Milwaukee Publishing Group, 1996, pp. 23-25
22. Ibid pp. 53-55
23. The LaFollettes of Wisconsin - Love and Politics in Progressive America by Bernard A. Weisberger, 1994, University of Wisconsin Press p. 36
24. Ibid p. 36
25. Ibid p. 45
26. Ibid p. 73
27. Ibid pp. 75-76
28. Ibid p. 135
29. Ibid pp. 52-53
30. Politics at the Periphery - Third Parties in Two-Party America by J. David Gillespie, University of South Carolina Press, 1993 p. 84
31. The LaFollettes of Wisconsin - Love and Politics in Progressive America by Bernard A. Weisberger, 1994, University of Wisconsin Press pp. 135-136
32. Ibid p. 184

33. Ibid pp. 185-186
34. Ibid p. 184
35. Ibid p. 186
36. Ibid p. 186
37. Ibid p. 191
38. Ibid p. 200
39. Ibid p. 205
40. Ibid pp. 203-204, 209
41. Ibid p. 212
42. The Almanac of American Politics 1988 by Michael Barone and Grant Ujifusa, National Journal, 1987, p. 1300
43. Milwaukee 150 - The Greater Milwaukee Story by Ellen Langhill and Dave Jensen, Milwaukee Publishing Group, 1996, pp. 67-69.
44. The LaFollettes of Wisconsin - Love and Politics in Progressive America by Bernard A. Weisberger, 1994, University of Wisconsin Press p. 210
45. Ibid p. 212
46. Lindbergh of Minnesota - A Political Biography, 1907-1918 by Bruce Larsen, Harcourt, Brace, Jovanvich, 1973 pp. 72-73
47. Ibid p. 45
48. Ibid p. 4
49. Ibid p. 216
50. Ibid p. 235
51. Ibid pp. 226-227.
52. Ibid p. 237
53. Ibid p. 226
54. The Populist Persuasion by Michael Kazin, Basic Books, 1995, p. 72
55. The LaFollettes of Wisconsin - Love and Politics in Progressive America by Bernard A. Weisberger, 1994, University of Wisconsin Press p. 242
56. Ibid pp. 229-230
57. Nye Committee information from Munitions Investigatory Committee webpage at website www.spartacus.schoolnet.co.uk/USAmic htm.

58. *The Cousins' Wars* - Religion, Politics, and the Triumph of Anglo-America by Kevin Phillips, Basic Books, 1999 p. 556

59. Minnesota's Farm-Laborism - The Third Party Alternative by Millard Gieske, University of Minnesota Press, 1979, p. 298

60. Dead Right by David Frum, Basic Books, p. 154

61. *The Cousins' Wars* - Religion, Politics, and the Triumph of Anglo-America by Kevin Phillips, Basic Books, 1999 p. 564

62. Politics at the Periphery - Third Parties in Two-Party America by J. David Gillespie, University of South Carolina Press, 1993 p. 89

63. The LaFollettes of Wisconsin - Love and Politics in Progressive America by Bernard A. Weisberger, 1994, University of Wisconsin Press p. 279

64. Ibid p. 300

65. Ibid p. 298

66. Ibid p. 302

67. Ibid p. 299

68. Ibid pp. 301-303

69. *Inter-County Leader* - stories found in various issues throughout 1944

70. The LaFollettes of Wisconsin - Love and Politics in Progressive America by Bernard A. Weisberger, 1994, University of Wisconsin Press p. 309

71. Interview with Robert Dueholm, June 18, 2004 at the offices of the *Inter-County Leader* in Frederic, Wisconsin

72. The LaFollettes of Wisconsin - Love and Politics in Progressive America by Bernard A. Weisberger, 1994, University of Wisconsin Press p. 313

73. Ibid p. 314

73. The Almanac of American Politics 1988 by Michael Barone and Grant Ujifusa, National Journal, 1987, p. 1284

74. The LaFollettes of Wisconsin - Love and Politics in Progressive America by Bernard A. Weisberger, 1994, University of Wisconsin Press p. 314

75. The *Inter-County Leader*, Nov. 4, 1948

CHAPTER 6

1. Free State Project website, www.freestateproject.com
2. "Why Conventions Are Scripted" by Sean Scallon, Etherzone website, www.etherzone.com, July 27, 2004
3. Interview with Jason P. Sorens, December 2004
4. The Almanac of American Politics 1988 by Michael Barone and Grant Ujifusa, National Journal, 1987, p. 480
5. Interview with Dr. J. Michael Hill, December, 2004
6. "Hickman, other officials switch to GOP; Demos name Young," by Walt Reichert, *Shelbyville Sentinel-News*, Dec. 22, 2004
7. "Finding the Right State for State's Rights," by Sean Scallon, *Chronicles: A Magazine of American Culture*, Vol. 27, No. 1, January, 2003, pp. 52-53
8. Interview with Jason P. Sorens, December, 2004
9. Interview with Thomas Naylor, December, 2004
10. Interview with Stephen Moore, December 2004
11. Interview with Ben Manski, December 2004
12. Interview with James Clymer, December 2004

Printed in the United States
45402LVS00005B/1-51